W9-ASO-666

Twayne's English Authors Series

EDITOR OF THIS VOLUME

Arthur F. Kinney
University of Massachusetts, Amherst

Lancelot Andrewes

TEAS 325

Lancelot Andrewes

John Payne's engraved frontispiece of Lancelot Andrewes for the Second Edition of Andrewes's XCVI Sermons (London, 1632)

LANCELOT ANDREWES

By TREVOR A. OWEN

Potomac State College of West Virginia University

TWAYNE PUBLISHERS
A DIVISION OF G. K. HALL & CO., BOSTON

Published in 1981 by Twayne Publishers,
A Division of G. K. Hall & Co.

Printed on permanent/durable acid-free paper and bound
in the United States of America

First Printing

Library of Congress Cataloging in Publication Data

Owen, Trevor A.
Lancelot Andrewes.

(Twayne's English authors series ; TEAS 325)
Bibliography: p. 170
Includes index.
1. Preaching—England–History.
2. Andrewes, Lancelot, 1555–1626.
I. Title. II. Series.
BV4208.G7079 251′.00942 81–2154
ISBN 0–8057–6769–X AACR2

This book is dedicated
to
the memory of
my mother and father

Contents

About the Author

Trevor Owen has taught at many colleges, including Wartburg College, Gustavus Adolphus College, The American University in Cairo, and Hampton Institute. He is presently an associate professor of English at Potomac State College of West Virginia University. His interest in the Renaissance period led him to found the Shakespeare and Renaissance Association of West Virginia. He has written articles and delivered papers on Shakespeare, Andrewes, and Donne, and he is currently working on a book on Bunyan's *Pilgrim's Progress*.

Preface

From the rich and varied tradition of almost five hundred years of English pulpit oratory, only the sermons of John Donne have received extensive attention in the twentieth century. Our age has seen a magnificent scholarly edition of Donne's collected sermons and numerous critical studies of his style and thought. By contrast, however, Lancelot Andrewes, the preacher whose star outshone Donne's in their own age, has received scant attention.

Indeed, it appears that Andrewes's sermons owe whatever attention they have received in the twentieth century to the influence of T. S. Eliot. It is even doubtful whether Andrewes would have been anthologized in the twentieth century if Eliot had not singled out one of his sermons (the second Wise Men sermon) for immortality, by quoting from it in the first five lines of his poem "The Journey of the Magi." Eliot also had enthusiastically praised Andrewes's thought and style in his essay "For Lancelot Andrewes," written in 1926, the three hundredth anniversary of Andrewes's death. But his words of praise were tempered with pessimism about Andrewes's reputation, and he prophesied that "Andrewes will never have many readers in any one generation, and his will never be the immortality of anthologies."

Eliot's gloomy prophecy appears to have been justified, because Andrewes's sermons have since received only meager attention from readers and scholars. I believe that this relative neglect is unfortunate, because the best of Andrewes's work ranks with the greatest prose of his age, and with the finest sermons in the language.

No extensive critical analysis of Andrewes's sermons has yet appeared, and my own book is designed partially to fill this gap. The first chapter traces the relevant facts of Andrewes's biography and attempts to determine the quality of his life. Chapter 2 discusses Andrewes's extensive prose works, besides the sermons; his religious works, particularly his *Catechism, Manual for the Sick,* and *Private Devotions*, provide an especially good introduction to his calling as a preacher. But the bulk of this book is devoted to Andrewes's sermons: Chapter 3 provides a general discussion of

Andrewes's characteristics as a preacher, and Chapters 4 through 9 present a critical analysis of the various groups of Andrewes's sermons. The last chapter summarizes Andrewes's intellectual achievement, contrasts his homiletic method with Donne's, briefly traces his reputation, and attempts to assess the enduring qualities of his genius.

In my study of Andrewes, I owe much to other scholars, and I have acknowledged my debts in the bibliography. I would like to call special attention, however, to certain works which should be helpful for those readers who would like to become more familiar with Andrewes's work. The best place to begin is with Eliot's famous essay, which still remains the finest introduction to Andrewes's achievement. Readers who wish to sample Andrewes's sermons will find the modern edition, by G.M. Story, of twelve of the best of his sermons enjoyable reading, and those who desire to read more widely may turn to the collected edition of Andrewes's sermons, conveniently reprinted by the AMS Press. Andrewes's devotional life has been beautifully revealed in the splendid edition of his *Private Devotions* by F. E. Brightman. And his life has been painstakingly reconstructed from numerous varied sources by Paul A. Welsby in his definitive biography.

I am most grateful to the many kind people who assisted me in procuring books essential for my study. I thank the staff of the Folger Shakespeare Library, in Washington, D.C., for their courteous assistance in allowing me to examine the earliest printed editions of Andrewes's sermons. Dr. Nati Krivatsy was especially helpful in efficiently preparing the way for my visit. I would also like to thank the staff of the British Museum Library, London, and the staffs of the following college libraries for their courteous efficiency in locating books, and making them accessible to me: the University of Minnesota, the University of West Virginia, Frostburg State College, and Potomac State College. I express my appreciation to Dr. Ruel Foster, of the English Department of West Virginia University, and to Dr. William Phipps, of the Religion and Philosophy Department of Davis and Elkins College, for their encouragement in the earliest stages of my work; and I thank Professor Arthur F. Kinney, G. K. Hall Field Editor, for his unusually thorough reading of my manuscript and for his valuable suggestions during the last stages of my book.

Like most authors, I owe a very personal debt of gratitude to my family. I thank my wife, Patricia, for her patience and her cheerful efficiency in typing the manuscript. And I thank my two sons, Alexander and Stephen, for giving up many hours and days with their father while he worked on his book.

TREVOR A. OWEN

Potomac State College

Chronology

1555 Lancelot Andrewes is born in Thames Street, London, the son of Thomas and Joan Andrewes.

ca. 1563 Sent to Cooper's Free School, London.

ca. 1565 Enters the Merchant Taylors' School, London.

1571 Enters Pembroke College, Cambridge, in September, at the age of sixteen. Named scholar of Jesus College, Oxford, although he does not take up residence.

1575 Receives the Bachelor of Arts Degree, February 4; later elected Fellow of Pembroke Hall.

1578 Granted the Master of Arts Degree from Pembroke College; appointed Catechist.

1580 Ordained deacon and made Junior Treasurer of Pembroke College.

1581 Made Senior Treasurer of Pembroke and incorporated at Jesus College, Oxford.

1585 Bachelor of Divinity Degree.

1586 Made Chaplain to Henry Hastings, the third Earl of Huntingdon, and accompanies him to the North, where "he converted recusants, priests, and others, to the Protestant religion." At about this time, appointed Chaplain in Ordinary to Queen Elizabeth, and Chaplain to John Whitgift, the Archbishop of Canterbury.

1588 Andrewes's first surviving sermon ("The Spittal Sermon") preached during Easter week, in the yard of Saint Mary's Hospital, London. At about this time, obtains his Doctor of Divinity Degree.

1589 Made vicar of Saint Giles, Cripplegate; Prebendary of Saint Paul's; and Prebendary of the Collegiate Church of Southwell; also elected Master of Pembroke Hall, September 6.

1590 Admitted to Gray's Inn, March 16. Appointed to visit the Separatist Henry Barrow, in Fleet Prison.

1591 With Dr. Alexander Nowell, Dean of Saint Paul's, appointed by the Lord Chancellor to confer in prison with the Puritan John Udal.

1593 Preaches at the opening of the Convocation of Canterbury, at Saint Paul's Cathedral, on February 20, attacking abuses in the clergy.

1594 Appointed a Commissioner to examine the conditions of the Ecclesiastical Courts in London.

1595 *The Judgment of the Lambeth Articles,* his first work of controversy, in Latin.

1597 Appointed by Queen Elizabeth, in March, to the Prebend of the Eleventh Stall of Westminster Abbey. On December 5, elected Treasurer of the Chapter.

1601 Appointed Dean of the Collegiate Church of Saint Peter, Westminster Abbey.

1603 Attends Queen Elizabeth's funeral in Westminster Abbey; assists at King James's coronation, July 25.

1604 Attends the Hampton Court Conference, convened by King James, in January; in July, commissioned as a translator of the Bible and made chairman of the Westminster Company of translators.

1605 Elevated to bishopric of Chichester; appointed Lord Almoner to the king.

1606 On November 5, preaches before the king at Whitehall, the first of his sermons commemorating England's day of deliverance from the Gunpowder Plot.

1609 *Tortura Torti* is published. Elected Bishop of Ely on September 27, confirmed on November 6, and consecrated on December 12.

1610 Present, on June 4, at the creation of Henry, James's son, Prince of Wales. *Responsio ad Apologiam Cardinalis Bellarmini* published. Begins friendship with Isaac Casaubon.

1613 Meets Hugo Grotius. Appointed by the king to a Commission investigating possible grounds for divorce between Lady Frances Howard and Robert Devereux, Earl of Essex.

1614 Confirms Casaubon's son, Meric; attends Casaubon's funeral.

1616 Appointed by the king as Privy Councillor, September 29. Present at the creation of James's son, Charles, Prince of Wales, November 3.

1617 Accompanies James I on his progress through Scotland; appointed Privy Councillor of Scotland, July 1.

1618 Appointed by the king to the bishopric of Winchester on July 20, and elected on August 3.

1619 Appointed Dean of the Chapels Royal. Present with the king at Royston, in March and April, during his sickness; attends Queen Anne's funeral on May 13.

1620 Entertains the king in August at his episcopal residence at Farnham Castle.

1621 Appointed to a committee on the bribery trial of Sir Francis Bacon; serves on a commission to investigate the charge of "casual homicide" brought against George Abbot, Archbishop of Canterbury.

1622 Again entertains the king at Farnham Castle, in August. On Christmas Day, preaches his second sermon on the Wise Men, his most famous work.

1623 On July 20, Andrewes administers to King James the oath supporting the Spanish Match between Prince Charles and Maria, the Spanish Infanta.

1624 On Christmas Day, preaches his last surviving sermon before James I at Whitehall.

1625 James I dies, but Andrewes's increasing sickness keeps him from preaching at court and attending the funeral.

1626 Carries the paten in the Coronation procession of King Charles I. Dies September 25; buried in Saint Saviour's Church, Southwark, on November 11.

1629 First collected edition of Andrewes's sermons appears, commissioned by Charles I.

CHAPTER 1

Andrewes's Life

LANCELOT Andrewes lived his quiet life during one of the most exciting periods of English history: his seventy–one years touched the reigns of the last two Tudor monarchs and the first two Stuarts. He gained his first renown as a preacher at the court of Elizabeth I (his first surviving sermon was preached in 1588, the year of the glorious English victory over the Spanish Armada) and he became *Stella Praedicantium* (the star of preachers) under King James I. His career is thus contemporaneous with Shakespeare's: on Christmas Day 1606, King James was listening to Andrewes preaching at the Chapel at Whitehall on the paradox of the *Verbum Infans*, and the next day he was being entertained at Whitehall by a performance of Shakespeare's *King Lear*. When Shakespeare died in 1616, Andrewes had not yet preached his greatest sermons, but his career in the pulpit was drawing to a close when the First Folio of Shakespeare's plays appeared in 1623.

Andrewes's earliest biographer declares that Andrewes speaks both "in his learned works and sermons" and "in his life and works of mercy,"[1] and his life does provide a valuable supplement to his writing. His biography is based on two main sources: the sermon preached at his funeral in 1626 by his friend John Buckeridge, Bishop of Rochester, and the brief biography entitled *An Exact Narration of the Life and Death of . . . Lancelot Andrewes* (1650), written by Henry Isaacson, Andrewes's secretary and friend. Facts of his life are also scattered throughout various seventeenth-century works: memoirs, letters, anecdotes, and biographical sketches.[2]

I *Family and Early Education*

Two years after the accession of Mary Tudor to the English throne, Lancelot Andrewes was born, in Thames Street, London, in the parish of All Hallows, Barking. The exact date of his birth is unknown, but he says in his *Devotions* that he was born on a Thursday. The name of his mother was apparently Joan and his father was Thomas Andrewes, mariner, descendant of an old Suffolk family. Lancelot was the first of thirteen children.

Buckeridge claims that Andrewes's " 'life was well composed and ordered even from his childhood.' I may well say of him as the prophet doth . . . 'Herein was his happiness, that he took up and did stoutly bear the yoke of the Lord even from his youth.' "[3] He was indeed fortunate in his early teachers. When he was about eight, he was sent to Cooper's Free School in Radcliffe; here the master Mr. Ward, recognizing the boy's abilities, persuaded his parents that he should not be apprenticed to a trade, and he was sent to the Merchant Taylors' School in London, whose headmaster was the famous Richard Mulcaster. Buckeridge declares that Master Ward and Master Mulcaster "contended for him, who should have the honour of his breeding, that after became the honour of their schools and all learning."[4] Andrewes's gratitude to his parents and his two earliest teachers was long-lasting: in his *Devotions* he prays for his "parents honest and good" and for his "teachers gentle."[5]

The most vivid account of Andrewes as a young scholar is also given by Buckeridge:

> his teachers and masters foresaw in him that he would prove *lumen literarum et literatorum*, "the burning and shining candle of all learning and learned men" . . . "he accounted all that time lost that he spent not in his studies," wherein in learning he outstripped all his equals, and his indefatigable industry had almost outstripped himself. He studied so hard when others played, that if his parents and masters had not forced him to play with them also, all the play had been marred. His late studying by candle, and early rising at four in the morning, procured him envy among his equals, yea with the ushers also, because he called them up too soon.[6]

II *College Years*

In September 1571, at the age of sixteen,[7] Andrewes entered Pembroke College, Cambridge, under one of the new Greek scholarships established by Dr. Thomas Watts, Archdeacon of Middlesex. In the same year he was named scholar of Jesus College, Oxford, which had recently been founded by the Welshman Hugh Price, although Andrewes never established residency there. In 1575 he received the Bachelor of Arts Degree from Pembroke College, and in 1576, having defeated a fellow student, Thomas Dove, in a scholastic trial, he was appointed Fellow of Pembroke Hall. In 1578 he was granted the Master of Arts Degree.

Andrewes's devotion to scholarship was evident at Cambridge, as it had been at the Merchant Taylors' School, although Buckeridge declares that in his intellectual achievements "he owed little to his tutors, but most to his own pains and study."[8] Isaacson relates "that within few years, he had laid the foundations of all arts and sciences, and had gotten skill in most of the modern languages."[9] In fact, Andrewes's interest in scholarship was so keen that he even utilized his Easter vacation visits to his parents: "his father, directed by letters from his son, before he came, prepared one that should read to him, and be his guide in the attaining of some language or art, which he had not attained before."[10] Isaacson also indicates that Andrewes's only physical activity was walking and that it was his custom during the Easter holiday to walk from Cambridge to his parents' house in London and back; he gave up this practice when he became Bachelor of Divinity because he was embarrassed that his friends believed "he had forborne riding only to save charges."[11] Isaacson also vividly describes Andrewes's love for the beauties of Nature, an enthusiasm which he would later reveal in some of the best passages of his sermons. Isaacson declares that Andrewes had been heard to say that

> he never loved or used any games or ordinary recreations, either within doors, as cards, dice, tables, chess, or the like; or abroad, as buts [putting], quoits, bowls, or any such: but his ordinary exercise and recreation was walking either alone by himself, or with some other selected companion, with whom he might confer and argue, and recount their studies; and he would often profess that to observe the grass, herbs, corn, trees, cattle, earth, waters, heavens, any of the creatures, and to contemplate their natures, orders, qualities, vırtues, uses, &c, was ever to him the greatest mirth, content, and recreation that could be: and this he held to his dying day.[12]

Andrewes was appointed Catechist of Pembroke College in 1578, and he delivered, at three o'clock on Saturdays and Sundays, a series of lectures on the Ten Commandments which were so popular that they attracted not only members of his own college but also students from other colleges and people from the surrounding countryside. A seventeenth-century editor of these lectures declared that "he was scarce reputed a pretender to learning and piety then in Cambridge, who made not himself a disciple of Mr. Andrewes by diligent resorting to his Lectures . . . and ever since they have in many hundreds of copies passed from hand to hand, and have been esteemed a very Library to young Divines, and an Oracle to consult at, to Laureat and grave Divines."[13] It was during Andrewes's service as catechist that a humorous experience supposedly occurred, recounted in an anecdote in John Aubrey's *Brief Lives*.

There was then at Cambridge a good fatt Alderman that was wont to sleep at Church, which the Alderman endeavoured to prevent but could not. Well! this was preached against as a signe of Reprobation. The good man was exceedingly troubled at it, and went to Andrewes his Chamber to be satisfied in point of Conscience. Mr. Andrewes told him, that it was an ill habit of Body, not of Mind, and that it was against his Will; advised him on Sundays to make a more sparing meale, and to mend it at Supper. The Alderman did so, but sleepe comes on again for all that, and was preached at; comes again to be resolved with teares in his eies. Andrewes then told him he would have him make a good heartie meal as he was wont to doe, and presently take out his full sleep. He did so, came to St. Maries, where the Preacher was prepared with a Sermon to damne all who slept at Sermon, a certain signe of Reprobation. The good Alderman, having taken his full nap before, lookes on the Preacher all Sermon time, and spoyled the design.[14]

Aubrey also relates an experience which Andrewes supposedly had with the Puritans of Emmanuel College.

The Puritan faction . . . had a great mind to drawe in this learned young man, whom (if they could make theirs) they knew would be a great honour to them. They carried themselves outwardly with great sanctity and strictnesse. They preached up very strict keeping and observing the Lord's day: made, upon the matter, damnation to breake it, and that 'twas less Sin to kill a man. Yet these Hyprocrites did bowle in a private green at their colledge every Sunday after Sermon; and one of the Colledge (a loving friend to Mr. L. Andrewes) to satisfie him, one time lent him the Key of a Private back dore to the bowling green, on a Sunday evening, which he opening, discovered these zealous Preachers with their Gownes off, earnest at play. But they were strangely surprised to see the entrey of one that was not of the Brotherhood.[15]

III *Recusants and Sectaries*

At Cambridge, Andrewes's fortunes continued to rise. In 1580 he was ordained deacon and made Junior Treasurer of Pembroke College; in 1581 he was made Senior Treasurer of Pembroke and incorporated Master of Arts at Jesus College, Oxford; and in 1585 he took the Bachelor of Divinity Degree. His reputation brought him to the attention of Henry Hastings, third Earl of Huntingdon, President of the North, and in 1586 Andrewes was made the Earl's Chaplain and accompanied him to the North where, according to Isaacson, "God so blessed his painful preachings, and moderate private conference, that he converted recusants, priests, and others, to the Protestant religion."[16]

He received his greatest benefits, however, from Sir Francis Walsingham, Secretary of State to Elizabeth. Walsingham had apparently shown interest in Andrewes when he was a boy, and while he was at Cambridge intended to make him Reader of Controversies, being determined, as Buckeridge declares, that "he would never permit him to take any country benefice, lest he and his great learning should be buried in a country church."[17] Walsingham wanted Andrewes to support the Puritan cause, according to Sir John Harington: "His patron (that studied projects of policy as much as precepts of piety) hearing of his fame, and meaning to make use thereof, sent for him . . . and dealt earnestly with him, to hold up a side that was even then falling, and to maintain certain state points of Puritanism. But he . . . answered him plainly, they were not only against his learning, but his conscience. The councillor . . . dismissed him with some disdain for the time; but afterward did the more reverence his integrity and honesty, and became no hinderer to his ensuing preferments."[18]

Andrewes never accepted the position of Reader of Controversies, but it was through the patronage of Walsingham that he was made vicar of Saint Giles, Cripplegate; Prebendary of Saint Pancras; and Prebendary of the Collegiate Church of Southwell, all in 1589.[19] His service as Confessor in the Prebend of Saint Paul's has also been noted by Harington: "While he held this place, his manner was, especially in Lent time, to walk duly at certain hours in one of the aisles of the church, that if any came to him for spiritual advice and comfort, (as some did, though not many,) he might impart it to them."[20] Andrewes's diligence in performing his new duties must have affected his health, and Isaacson declares that "he became so infirm, that his friends despaired of his life."[21] He was elected Master of Pembroke Hall on September 6, 1589, upon the death of William Fulke.

The 1590s brought Andrewes widening responsibilities and increasing honors. In 1590 he and forty-one other preachers were appointed by the Bishop of London, at the order of Archbishop John Whitgift, to visit imprisoned sectaries with the hope of persuading them to reject their unorthodox beliefs. Andrewes and a Mr. Hutchinson visited in Fleet Prison the Separatist Henry Barrow, who, among his other unorthodoxies, had refused to take the Oath of Supremacy. Andrewes visited Barrow on March 18 and April 13. At their first meeting, a long discussion was climaxed by Andrewes's witty comment that Barrow's imprisonment gave him the opportunity for "the solitary and contemplative life." But Barrow responded with a rebuke: "You speak philosophically, but not Christianly."[22] Andrewes was unable to persuade Barrow to recant and three years later, on April 6, 1593, he and his fellow Separatist John Greenwood were hanged at Tyburn.

In 1591, Andrewes was appointed along with Doctor Alexander Nowell, Dean of Saint Paul's, to confer with the Puritan John Udal, who had been accused and imprisoned for writing seditiously against the bishops during the Martin Marprelate controversy. Although Udal enjoyed the visits of Andrewes, he refused to recant. He was pardoned in 1592, but died in prison before he could be released.

Not only did Andrewes seek to bring heretics back into the fold, but he was also concerned with strengthening the Church from within. At the opening of the Convocation of Canterbury on February 20, 1593, he preached a powerful sermon in Latin attacking the abuses in the Church. In 1594, he was appointed by Archbishop Whitgift as a commissioner to examine the conditions of the Ecclesiastical Courts in London. And in 1595 he wrote, in Latin, his first work of controversy, *The Judgment of the Lambeth Articles*, his response to the extreme Calvinism of the Nine Articles, a work commissioned by Archbishop Whitgift but one offensive to the queen.

IV *Dean of Westminster*

Elizabeth I favored Andrewes; Isaacson declares that she "took . . . delight in his preaching and grave deportment."[23] He frequently preached at court, and served the queen as one of her chaplains in ordinary, although he declined bishoprics she offered him.[24] Yet it was also the queen who brought about his first association with Westminster, when in March 1597 she appointed him to the Prebend of the Eleventh Stall of Westminster Abbey. On December 5, 1597, he was elected Treasurer of the Chapter, a position he held for little more than a year. In July 1601 Sir Robert Cecil, Lord High Steward of Westminster, nominated Andrewes Dean of the Collegiate Church of Saint Peter, Westminster Abbey. Thus brought into association with Westminster School, he developed a relationship with the boys which was described in later years by Bishop John Hacket, one of his students, in an anecdote revealing Andrewes's devotion to scholarship as well as his humanity.

> I told him [Archbishop Williams] how strict that excellent man was to charge our masters that they should give us lessons out of none but the most classical authors; that he did often supply the place both of the head schoolmaster and usher for the space of an whole week together, and gave us not an hour of loitering time from morning to night; how he caused our exercises in prose and verse to be brought to him, to examine our style and proficiency. That he never walked to Chiswick for his recreation without a brace of this young fry, and in that wayfaring leisure had a singular dexterity to fill those narrow vessels with a funnel. And, which was the greatest burden of his toil, sometimes thrice in a week, sometimes oftener, he sent for the uppermost scholars to his lodgings at night, and kept them with him from eight till eleven, unfolding to them the best rudiments of the Greek tongue, and the elements of the Hebrew grammar; and all this he did to boys without any compulsion of correction; Nay I never heard him utter so much as a word of austerity among us.[25]

V *Andrewes and King James I*

Following the death of Queen Elizabeth on March 24, 1603, Andrewes's fortunes improved still more under James I. Isaacson declares that the "most learned King James" admired Andrewes "beyond all other divines" for his preaching and his learning,[26] and Andrewes was soon preaching at the Royal Chapel at Whitehall on the holy days of the Church. Andrewes was also invited by the king to attend the Hampton Court Conference from January 14 to 16, 1604. The conference had been called by the king in response to a petition of Puritan ministers who sought a reorganization of the church; during many subsequent discussions Andrewes, according to the records, spoke out only once, on the second day, concerning the use of the sign of the Cross in Baptism. When he was asked about the tradition, he replied, "It appears out of Tertullian, Cyprian, and Origen, and it was used in *immortali lavacro*."[27]

The Hampton Court Conference resulted in plans for a new English translation of the Bible; forty-seven scholars set to work on it. The task was divided among six companies, and Andrewes was chosen chairman of the Westminster Company and charged with the responsibility of translating Genesis through Second Kings. (His brother Roger served on one of the Cambridge committees.) The translation was not completed until 1611. Although posterity has placed great importance on the King James Bible, neither Buckeridge nor Isaacson mentions Andrewes's work as translator; and it is interesting that, in Andrewes's sermons delivered after 1611, he relies not on the new verson, but on the Latin Vulgate and the English Geneva Bible.

During the reign of Elizabeth, Andrewes had been offered the bishoprics of Salisbury and Ely, but he had refused them because he disapproved of the custom of turning over, upon acceptance, part of the revenues of the see to the Crown. This practice was declared illegal by James's first Parliament, and when Andrewes was offered the bishopric of Chichester by the king, he was free to accept. He was elected on October 16, 1605, confirmed on October 31, and consecrated on November 3. According to Isaacson, Andrewes accepted this new honor with humility: "he caused to be engraven about the seal of his Bishopric, those words of St. Paul, *Et ad haec quis idoneus?* 'And who is sufficient for these things?' "[28] He was also appointed Lord Almoner to the King. He resigned, probably on November 5, the mastership of Pembroke Hall, officially bringing to a close his long and distinguished career at Cambridge; and he also relinquished the deanery of Westminster and the vicarage of Saint Giles. He was, however, allowed to keep the prebend at Saint Paul's, which he held until his translation to the bishopric of Ely in 1609.

VI *The Gunpowder Plot and Its Consquences*

On the day of Andrewes's consecration, November 3, a letter revealing the Gunpowder Plot was shown to the king. If the plot had been successful, the king and members of Parliament would have been blown up at the opening of Parliament on November 5, and Andrewes, as a new bishop, would also have been present and undoubtedly killed. The memory of the plot profoundly influenced Andrewes's imagination for the rest of his life. Ten of his surviving sermons commemorate the deliverance on November 5, the anniversary of the plot, and in his other sermons he refers to it more often than to any other contemporary event.

The discovery of the plot indirectly brought about Andrewes's most important works of controversy. The threat to James led almost at once to an Oath of Allegiance. Pope Paul V, in two breves of 1606 and 1607, ordered English Catholics to abstain from taking the oath; King James defended the oath in his *Apology for the Oath of Allegiance*, published in 1608; and the famous controversialist Cardinal Roberto Bellarmine, using the assumed name of his chaplain, responded to the king in the same year in his *Responsio Matthaei Torti*. James I replied to Bellarmine, but he also commissioned Andrewes to answer the cardinal. Andrewes's *Tortura Torti* was published in June 1609; Bellarmine, in his *Apology for the Responsio Torti*, responded to Andrewes's work; and Andrewes, in turn, answered with the *Responsio ad Apologiam Cardinalis Bellarmini*, published in 1610. These two Latin pieces represent Andrewes's most extensive work. Although the role of controversialist was probably uncongenial to him, his labors were appreciated, and Isaacson declares that the king selected Andrewes "as his choicest piece, to vindicate his regality against his foulmouthed adversaries."[29]

VII *Andrewes and the King: Later Honors*

In 1609, the same year as the publication of *Tortura Torti*, Andrewes was recommended by the king to the bishopric of Ely. He was elected on September 27, confirmed on November 6, and enthroned on December 12. Andrewes was so popular with the king that when Richard Bancroft, Archbishop of Canterbury, died in 1610, many of the clergy doubtless expected that Andrewes would be the king's choice to fill that vacancy, but the king appointed George Abbot instead, declaring that he had reached his decision in order to fulfill a promise made to his good friend the late George Home, Earl of Dunbar.

Two years later, in 1613, Abbot and Andrewes were called together for an event which was the only major blemish in Andrewes's public life. On May 16, the king appointed a commission of Abbot, Andrewes, three other bishops, and six laymen to inquire into the validity of the marriage between Lady Frances Howard and Robert Devereaux, Earl of Essex, and to investigate possible grounds for divorce. Because of the king's infatuation with Robert Carr, Viscount Rochester, who wished to marry Lady Frances, James openly favored the divorce and attempted to influence the judgment of his commissioners. It is ironic that Abbot, whom the king had made archbishop two years previously, remained firm against the king's wishes, while Andrewes, who had been passed over, was apparently persuaded by the king to support him. On September 25 the commission decided in favor of the divorce. Lady Frances and Viscount Rochester married, but were later disgraced when implicated in the murder of Sir Thomas Overbury.

Andrewes's personality must have been congenial to his sovereign, and it has been reported that "his gravity in a manner awed King James, who refrained from that mirth and liberty in the presence of this prelate, which otherwise he assumed to himself."[30] Andrewes's fortunes continued to be closely bound up with the favors of the king, and he was frequently with James on important occasions. He accompanied James I on his state visit to Cambridge in March 1615, when he probably first met the young George Herbert. Andrewes was appointed Privy Councillor of England on September 29, 1616,[31] and, in the same year, on November 3, he was present at the creation of James's son Charles as Prince of Wales. When the king made his unpopular progress through Scotland (March through September 1617) with the vain hope of imposing the English ritual on the Scottish kirk, Andrewes accompanied him, preached the Pentecost sermon at Holyrood-House in Edinburgh on June 8, and was declared, upon James's instigation, Privy Councillor of Scotland on July 1. One year later, on July 20, 1618, Andrewes was nominated for the bishopric of Winchester; he was elected on August 3, although he did not take up residence until the spring of 1619. On January 1, 1619, Andrewes was made Dean of the Chapels Royal, and upon appointment to that position he surrendered his office as Royal Almoner. In March, Queen Anne died, and Andrewes was present at her funeral on May 13. Twice, in August 1620 and in August 1622, Andrewes elaborately entertained the king at his episcopal residence at Farnham Castle. A friend of Andrewes, John Chamberlain, noted that for the first entertainment of three days it cost Andrewes about £2,300 or £2,400.[32]

VIII *Francis Bacon and George Abbot*

In 1621 Andrewes participated in the proceedings associated with the misfortunes of two prominent men: Francis Bacon, Lord Chancellor, and George Abbot, Archbishop of Canterbury. As a peer of the House of Lords, Andrewes took part in the bribery trial of Bacon, although he had been a personal friend of Bacon's for many years. On March 21 Andrewes was appointed to serve on one of three committees to investigate witnesses; on April 30 he was on a committee of twelve peers who visited Bacon to ascertain whether he acknowledged the confession which had been made in his name in the House of Lords; and on June 10 he was present at the delivery of the Great Seal to John Williams, Dean of Westminster, who succeeded Bacon as Lord Keeper.

Later in 1621 Andrewes sat on a commission with six bishops and four laymen to investigate the case of the Archbishop of Canterbury, George Abbot, who during a hunting party in October had accidentally shot a groom, Peter Hawkins. The commission debated whether or not there were any irregularities in this "casual homicide." Andrewes was apparently the only one of the six bishops who strongly supported Abbot, and he appears magnanimous in defending the archbishop against his accusers: "Brethren . . . be not too busy to condemn any for uncanonicals according to the strictness thereof, lest we render ourselves in the same condition."[33] Abbot was subsequently cleared by the commission and absolved by the king.

IX *Andrewes and the King: The Last Years*

In Andrewes's position as Privy Councillor he never opposed the king on any matter of public policy. He apparently supported the king in 1623 in the latter's desire for a match between his son Prince Charles and the Spanish Infanta, and on July 20 he administered the oath to the king upholding the marriage. The ceremony never took place, but an interesting account survives which describes Andrewes's prophecy of Charles's future faithfulness to the Church. Shortly after the prince's return from Spain, Matthew Wren, a chaplain who had accompanied Charles, was called to Winchester House, Andrewes's residence, and was there confronted by Andrewes, the Bishop of Durham (Dr. Neile), and the Bishop of Saint David's (Dr. Laud), who asked Wren how his master stood to the Church of England. At the end of this discussion Andrewes is reputed to have made the following prophecy: "I am sure I shall be a true prophet: I shall be in my grave, and so shall you, my Lord of Durham; but my Lord of David's, and you, Doctor, will live to see that day that your master will be put to it, upon his head, and his crown, without he will forsake the support of the Church."[34] This anecdote provides such an accurate "prophecy" that it gives the appearance of having been fabricated after the fact.

The last recorded exchange between Andrewes and his sovereign is reported in an anecdote which relates a conversation which supposedly took place among the king, Andrewes, and Bishop Neile in 1624, at a dinner on the day the king dismissed his last Parliament. The king asked if he could not take his subjects' money without consulting Parliament. Neile replied, "God forbid, Sir, but you shou'd, you are the Breath of our Nostrils." And when the king turned to Andrewes, he responded, with characteristic wit, "Sir, I think it's lawful for you to take my Brother Neal's money, for he offers it."[35]

When James I was dying, his thoughts turned naturally to Andrewes. On March 24, 1625 (ironically, the anniversary of the king's accession), he called for Andrewes to pray with him and to administer the Sacrament, but Andrewes was himself too sick with the gout and the stone to attend. Andrewes's sickness also prevented him from attending the king's funeral on May 7. Perhaps it was Andrewes's poor health which explains the fact that he never preached at the court of James's successor, Charles I. Buckeridge declares in his funeral sermon for Andrewes that when Andrewes's "weakness grew on him, and that by infirmity of his body he grew unable to preach, he began to go little to the Court, not so much for weakness as for inability to preach."[36]

Andrewes's last days have also been vividly described by Buckeridge.

> After the death of his brother Master Thomas Andrewes in the sickness time, whom he loved dearly, he began to foretel his own death before the end of summer or before the beginning of winter. And when his brother Master Nicholas Andrewes died, he took that as a certain sign and prognostic and warning of his own death, and from that time till the hour of his dissolution he spent all his time in prayer; and his prayer-book, when he was private, was seldom seen out of his hands; and in the time of his fever and last sickness, besides the often prayers which were read to him, in which he repeated all the parts of the Confession and other petitions with an audible voice, as long as his strength endured, he did—as was well observed by certain tokens in him—continually pray to himself, though he seemed otherwise to rest or slumber; and when he could pray no longer *voce*, "with his voice," yet *oculis et manibus*, "by lifting up his eyes and hands" he prayed still; and when *nec manus nec vox officium faciunt*, "both

voice, and eyes, and hands failed" in their office, then *corde*, "with his heart," he still prayed, until it pleased God to receive his blessed soul to Himself.[37]

Lancelot Andrewes died in Winchester House on September 25, 1626; he was given an elaborate funeral on November 11; and he was buried in the upper aisle of the parish church of St. Saviour's in Southwark. "He is now at rest and peace in heaven," declared Buckeridge, and " 'follows the Lamb wheresoever He goes.' "[38]

X *The Quality of the Life*

From the many facts and anecdotes of the life of Lancelot Andrewes there appear vivid flashes revealing the man: the schoolboy studying late into the night; the young college student walking the English countryside, enjoying the beauties of Nature; the catechist good-naturedly giving advice to a fat alderman; the dean sharing his learning with the "brace of young fry" following at his heels; the preacher kindly looking over the sermon-notes of his chaplains; the bishop wittily responding to his sovereign; and the dying Christian breathing out his last prayers.

The quality of Andrewes's life also emerges, although more slowly. Buckeridge refers to Andrewes as a "text that lies before us . . . 'a man whose worth may not be passed over in silence,' whom all ages with us may celebrate and admire,"[39] and it is clear that the life presented by both Buckeridge and Isaacson is a saint's life, free from error or sin. But his life was not perfect, and modern biographers have attempted to present a more complete picture by calling attention to his weaknesses, especially his moral lapse in the Essex divorce proceedings, in which he allowed his conscience to be overmastered by the influence of his king, and his nepotism in bestowing offices on his unworthy brother Roger.

Perhaps, though, the quality of life which Andrewes sought and found is best indicated by his own words. When he visited the Separatist Henry Barrow in prison, he jokingly declared, "you are most happy. The solitary and contemplative life I hold the most blessed life. It is the life I would choose."[40] Like most humor, this statement contains the kernel of truth, and the words could describe Andrewes's own life, since it was, to a degree, "solitary" and "contemplative" and almost entirely "blessed." The only turbulent experience in his life was the frightening realization that he came near death with the Gunpowder Plot of 1605. Andrewes never married or traveled abroad. His serene life provides a contrast with the troubled early years of his contemporary churchman John Donne: whereas Donne frantically sought secular advancement, and fought off until the last moment a career in the Church, Andrewes was certain of his calling, even as a young man, and his life proceeded happily from honor to honor with no significant impediments or frustrations. Andrewes's peaceful life does not coincide with the romantic stereotype of the Renaissance man which we have reconstructed in our time. Not all men of the English Renaissance, however, were perturbed spirits like Nashe, Marlowe, Bacon, and Donne, Andrewes's contemporaries. There were also great spirits like Andrewes who were calm, contemplative men, but who were, nevertheless, completely characteristic of the quiet devotional spirit of their age.

Andrewes obviously did prefer the life of solitary contemplation to the turbulent life of political service. Buckeridge declares that Andrewes "spake and meddled little in civil and temporal affairs, being out of his profession and element; but in causes that any way concerned the Church and his calling he spake fully and home to the purpose."[41] A later tradition relates that when Andrewes came to the Council Chamber he would ask, "Is there anything to be done today for the Church?" If there was, he would remain; if not, he would depart.[42] Although Andrewes held many important public offices and served on numerous committees and commissions, he apparently never spoke out on public issues.

Andrewes's life, then, was balanced. Although it is reported that he spent almost five hours each day in prayer,[43] he did not flee from the world, and he loved the fellowship of men. Isaacson, with words similar in spirit to Chaucer's description of the Franklin, praises Andrewes's hospitality: "His table being ever bountifully and neatly furnished with provisions, and attendants answerable; to whom he committed the care of providing and expending in a plentiful yet orderly way; himself seldom knowing what meat he had, till he came from his study to dinner, at which he would show himself so noble in his entertainment, and so gravely facetious, that his guests would often profess, they never came to any man's table where they received better satisfaction in all points, and that his Lordship kept Christmas all the year, in respect of the plenty they ever found there."[44] Indeed, Andrewes's involvement with life may be partially gauged by noting the many famous men of the age who esteemed him or were his friends. Early in his life, the writers John Lyly and Thomas Nashe admired his preaching. Francis Bacon sought his advice on prose style, dedicated to him his *Holy War*, and declared that he held him in special reverence. The world-renowned scholar Isaac Casaubon was a great admirer and an intimate friend. And the churchman Richard Hooker, the antiquarian William Camden, the poet George Herbert,[45] and the church leader William Laud were all his associates.

In a beautiful passage from one of his Resurrection sermons, on the text "Set your affection on things above not on things on the earth," Andrewes nicely weighs the claims of this world and the next: "never seek for true glory here: why? *Locus est pulicum et culicum*, 'It is the place of fleas and gnats this.' In the garden, the place of our delight, we meet with worms; and there be spiders even in the King's palace. This place of worms and spiders, call ye this the place of glory in dust and cobwebs? . . . They that are in glory have not the quietest life; and they that are most at rest, farthest off from being glorious. Rest is here a thing inglorious, and glory a thing restless."[46] The beauty of Andrewes's life is that he was, indeed, able to combine these seemingly contradictory qualities of rest and glory, and to keep in balance the life of contemplation and the life of service. And it was in his divine calling of preacher that this balance was most vividly revealed. His sermons were created in the spirit of rest and contemplation, they were delivered for the spiritual enlightenment of his fellow Christians, and they earned him the glory of being honored as one of the greatest preachers of his age. If ever a man was happy in his calling and ideally suited for his profession, it was Lancelot Andrewes. Not only did he seek both rest and glory in the life to come, but he also found them in his earthly life of "dust and cobwebs."

CHAPTER 2

The Minor Works

I *The Works of Controversy*

ALTHOUGH Andrewes's fame was won in the pulpit, he also distinguished himself in his own age as a religious controversialist. His first work of controversy, *The Judgment of the Lambeth Articles*, composed in Latin in 1595, was written in response to the Nine Articles on the subject of predestination and election which had been commissioned by Archbishop Whitgift and written by William Whitaker and Henry Tindal. The work is brief (only eleven pages in the modern edition), consisting of the complete text of the Articles, together with Andrewes's responses;[1] the first known date of publication is 1660.

The *Judgment* is too tentative to be considered an important work. In his brief introduction, Andrewes refers to the topic of predestination and reprobation as a "great deep," and he declares that he has never disputed these controversial points since he was made a priest sixteen years previously. His responses to the Nine Articles are not so much refutations of the doctrines of predestination and election as qualifications of the extreme Calvinist position. For example, in responding to the First Article's declaration that God has from all eternity predestined some to life and reprobated others to death, Andrewes does not deny God's foreknowledge or that some are predestined to life through Christ, but he does declare that some are reprobate through their own sins, emphasizing personal responsibility rather than divine influence. He appears to vacillate, however, when he declares that those whom God did not choose he reprobated.

Andrewes also appears to waver in discussing the equally perplexing topic of whether or not the elect can be assured of their salvation. He agrees with the Articles that a true living faith will not fail in the elect, but he vacillates on the question of whether the Holy Spirit can be removed or extinguished. This feeling of uncertainty appears in several of Andrewes's responses, and the work as a whole contributes nothing to a clarification of these confusing topics. Perhaps Andrewes's own frustration may be detected in his concluding words, recommending silence to Christians on these disputed points.

Andrewes discusses the doctrine of election again in a brief work entitled *Censure of the Censure upon Barrett*,[2] written in Latin about the same time as the *Judgment*. William Barrett, Fellow of Gonville and Caius College, Cambridge, had attacked the Puritan position on the subject of predestination and election, and he had been forced to recant by Archbishop Whitgift. The *Censure* supports Barrett's belief that "no man ought to be absolutely secure as to his salvation."[3]

Fourteen years later, in 1609, Andrewes wrote, again in Latin, a far more ambitious work of controversy: the *Tortura Torti*. This work was inspired by the dispute between the papacy and James I over the Oath of Allegiance, which the king had instituted in the aftermath of the Gunpowder Conspiracy; Andrewes was commissioned by the king to answer Roberto Bellarmine, who had served Pope Paul V in answering the king, a task Andrewes fulfilled in the *Tortura Torti*. Andrewes's work extends to 496 pages in the modern edition.[4]

Tortura Torti suggests that Andrewes found the role of controversialist uncongenial. His friend John Chamberlain, commented on Andrewes's difficulty in a letter, declaring that "we say that the bishop of Chichester [Andrewes] is appointed to aunswer Bellarmin about the oth of allegeaunce, which taske I doubt how he will undertake and performe, beeing so contrarie to his disposition and course to meddle with controversies."[5] The king's interference must have been troublesome to Andrewes as well, for Chamberlain remarks, in another letter, "I doubt he [Andrewes] be not at leysure for any by-matters, the King doth so hasten and spurre him on in this busines of Bellarmine: which he were like to perform very well . . . yf he might take his own time, and not be troubled nor intangled with arguments obtruded to him continually by the Kinge."[6] Even the French ambassador was aware of Andrewes's difficulties, referring to Andrewes's work as "a web of Penelope."[7]

The main attack of *Tortura Torti* is on what Andrewes regarded as excessive powers of the papacy, especially the pope's claims to depose monarchs and to absolve subjects from oaths of allegiance.

The papacy based its claims to power on Jesus' words to Peter: "and whatsoever thou shalt bind on earth shall be bound in heaven: and whatsoever thou shalt loose on earth shall be loosed in heaven" (Matthew 16:19). In presenting the papacy's interpretation of these words, Andrewes ironically declares that the pope regards "binding" as binding men to guilt and treason, and "loosing" as loosing men from the bonds of law, duty, and faith. And he bitterly affirms that the pope certainly could not intend the powers of loosing to loosen man's allegiance to the laws of nature, which include the duty of civil obedience, the laws of the Ten Commandments, and the evangelical laws in which are found the words of Peter himself: "Be ye subject to the King as supreme: for this is the will of God" (I Peter 2:13, 15). Certainly, Andrewes declares, Paul V does not regard himself as equal with Peter. And just as a man who binds himself to keep the seventh commandment against adultery cannot be released from his oath by a pope, neither can a man who binds himself to the civil obedience ordered by the fifth commandment be absolved from his oath.[8]

Andrewes also attacks the papacy for misapplying its authority, declaring that it exercises power not when souls are endangered but when tenths are refused and sales of indulgences forbidden. Its aim is not the glory of God but the dishonor of princes, not the salvation of souls but the wasting of their substance; and once this aim is achieved, the glory of God and the salvation of souls may go where they please.[9] The power of the papal bulls has had disastrous effects in England. The brief issued against King James was, in effect, a sanctification of the Gunpowder Conspiracy, as the bull published by Pope Pius V against Elizabeth had transformed loyal Catholic subjects into recusants who refused to attend the established worship.[10]

Andrewes is skeptical about the doctrine of papal supremacy and its claims of direct succession of popes from Saint Peter. Turning to history, Andrewes accuses the papacy of schism and heresy; and he presents vivid examples of the papacy's involvement in sordid murders.[11] In playing with the name of the present pope, Paul V, he even claims to find the number of the beast and Anti-Christ, 666, from the Book of Revelation: PaVlo V. VICe Deo.[12]

Although much of the *Tortura Torti* directly assaults the papacy, some passages present a positive defense of the Church of England. Andrewes turns Bellarmine's charge of sacrilege back on him, attacking the Catholics' prayers in a foreign language, their denial of the Cup to the laity, and their worship of images. But it is Andrewes's response to Bellarmine's accusation of novelty that bears his most eloquent defense of the English Church: "Our religion you miscall modern sectarian opinions. I tell you if they are modern, they are not ours; our appeal is to antiquity . . . We do not innovate; it may be we *renovate* what was customary with those same ancients, but with you has disappeared in novelties."[13]

Bellarmine responded to Andrewes's *Tortura Torti* in his *Apologia pro Responsione sua* (1610), and Andrewes replied in his *Responsio ad Apologiam Cardinalis Bellarmine* (also 1610). The *Responsio* is even longer than the *Tortura* (500 pages in the modern edition). Andrewes's friend the great scholar Isaac Casaubon, who had just arrived in England from France, read the *Responsio* in manuscript and made corrections. In his diary, Casaubon expresses enthusiasm for Andrewes's work, declaring, "I had dinner today with the Bishop of Ely and heard him read chapter VIII of his book. It is wonderful with what elegance this most learned man confutes the theological scum, the folly, and sometimes the impious blasphemies of Bellarmine."[14] Andrewes himself was disappointed with Bellarmine's *Apologia*, and his friend Chamberlain declares in a letter that Andrews "thincks that either the man is much crased from that he was, or els that he did yt with a contemptuous negligence."[15] Andrewes in fact begins his *Responsio* with an attack on the style and structure of Bellarmine's work, declaring that his adversary's fighting days are over.[16]

The *Responsio* is composed of seventeen chapters. Like the *Tortura Torti*, it is both an attack on what Andrewes regards as the excessive claims of the papacy and a defense of the Church of England. Bellarmine had rejected the right of any man to be called "Catholic" who denied transubstantiation, the temporal claims of the papacy, and the invocation of saints. As reply, Andrewes declares that his Church regards the Eucharist as a sacrifice, but he directly challenges the Roman Catholic position: "Do you take away from the Mass your Transubstantiation; and there will not be any strife with us about the Sacrifice. Willingly we allow that a memory of the Sacrifice is made there. That your Christ made of bread is sacrificed there we will never allow."[17] In discussing the Eucharist Andrewes declares that his church does not define the mode of the Sacrament, but leaves it with the mode of the Incarnation, as a mystery.[18] With respect to the Roman belief in the invocation of saints, Andrewes, with Origen, places the idea in the category of "the hidden things of God."[19]

Andrewes proudly claims the title "Catholic" for the English Church, declaring that it is closer to the spirit of the Primitive Church than the Romans are. The English Church has merely cleansed itself of the filth of history and restored the form which the faith originally possessed, and he confidently affirms that it is to this reformed faith that his church clings, not to the Roman Catholic deformation of it.

Against the temporal claims of the papacy, Andrewes upholds the claims of royal supremacy. His appeal is to history: to the Jewish kings, Christian emperors, and former kings of England. He rejects both the belief that the state is subject to the Church and the papal claim that Peter had supremacy over the other apostles. In fact, he contrasts the pride of the popes with the humility of Saint Peter. Pope Paul V presented his foot to be kissed by royal legates; Peter, however, had declared to the Roman centurion, "I also am a man" (Acts 10:26).[20] The pope claims that kings are subject to the papacy, whereas Peter had admonished Christians to "submit to every ordinance of man for the Lord's sake, whether it be to the king as supreme" (I Peter 2:13). Andrewes confidently insists that the keys were never given to Peter to build the Church on the ruins of the state.[21]

The bulk of the *Responsio* is a defense of the Church of England addressed to the Roman Catholic Church, but the work also presents, in one passage, Andrewes's most extensive discussion of Puritanism. He does not object to the Puritans' doctrine, but to their discipline:

> for they have *no distinct and peculiar religion*, but discipline. And this I would have applied (not to the Scotch only but) to *the Puritans generally*, and to those among them who, except they are too violently addicted to their order of church government, are in other things sufficiently sober-minded; and these, however infatuated in their devotedness to their "*platform*," are yet *sufficiently orthodox in the rest of their doctrine*. . . . But with me they are *Puritans* from their exterior form of *discipline*, but not from their *religion*, which both is the same and can be, where the external face of discipline is not the same.[22]

The *Tortura Torti* and the *Responsio* are Andrewes's major works of controversy, but he also presented his beliefs on various religious questions in other miscellaneous works. He continues his discussion of issues raised in the *Tortura Torti* and the *Responsio*, for instance, in his *Two Answers to Cardinal Perron*. The cardinal had been engaged in a friendly controversy with Andrewes, Casaubon, and King James on the subject of what distinguishes a true Catholic; and Andrewes was asked by the king to reply to the cardinal's responses, which had been published after his death. In answering the cardinal, Andrewes finds the Church of England in agreement with the Roman Catholic Church on many beliefs. He affirms that the Eucharist is both a Sacrament and a Sacrifice; and he admits, in discussing the subject of prayers for the dead, that "there is little to be said against it; it cannot be denied, but that it is ancient."[23] However, he rejects the Roman Catholic denial of the Cup to the laity and their belief in the invocation of saints.

A Discourse Against Second Marriage is a brief tract, written in 1601, taking a conservative position on the question of divorce. Andrewes declares that "the act of adultery doth not dissolve the bond of marriage" and that "second marriages (where either party is living) are not warranted by the word of God."[24] The bond of marriage is broken only by death.

Two of the speeches survive which Andrewes delivered in the Star Chamber when he was Privy Councillor. In June 1618 he spoke to the Countess of Shrewsbury, who had been called to the Star Chamber because she refused to reveal what she knew about the relationship of her niece, Arabella Stuart, with William Seymour. She argued that she had taken a vow of silence on the subject, but Andrewes replied that her vow was no true oath and so should be broken.[25] On another occasion in the same year he spoke against John Traske, who had been called to the Chamber for preaching Judaizing beliefs. In Andrewes's brief speech he attacks Traske for his belief that Christians should abstain from the meats prohibited Jews in the Book of Leviticus and for his contention that Christians are bound to observe the Jewish Sabbath. The whole speech is well structured. It begins with a forceful attack on Traske's position: "It is a good work to make a Jew a Christian: but to make Christian men Jews, hath ever been holden a foul act, and severely to be punished."[26] It then proceeds with thorough citations of Scripture against Traske's opinions, concluding with a powerful anathema.

In the *Letters to Peter Du Moulin*, a French Huguenot, written in 1618, Andrewes supports the superiority of bishops over priests by divine right; he emphasizes that this belief is not a matter of faith but of practice. In a frequently quoted passage from his second letter, he expresses beautifully his spirit of tolerance for diversity in Christian practice:

Nevertheless, if our form be of divine right, it does not follow from thence that there is no salvation without it, or that a church cannot stand without it. He is blind who does not see churches standing without it; he must be hard hearted who denies them salvation. We are not of these hard-hearted persons; we put a great difference between these things. Something may be lacking in the exterior regiment, which is of divine right, and yet salvation to be had. . . . To prefer a better is not to condemn a thing. It is not to condemn your church if we recall it to another form, namely our own, which the better agrees with all antiquity.[27]

Although succeeding generations have all but forgotten Andrewes's controversial works, his own age appreciated this aspect of his writings.[28] It was Sir John Harington who spoke most eloquently of Andrewes's talents as a controversialist, expressing the highest hopes for the future: "I persuade myself, that whensoever it shall please God to give the King means, with consent of his confederate princes, to make that great peace which His blessed word, *Beati pacifici*, seemeth to promise,—I mean the ending of this great schism in the Church of God, procured as much by ambition as superstition,—this reverend prelate will be found one of the ablest, not of England only, but of Europe, to set the course for composing the controversies."[29]

II The Pattern of Catechistical Doctrine

The quality of Lancelot Andrewes's religious life is revealed not only in his sermons but also in his other religious works; and *The Pattern of Catechistical Doctrine*, *The Manual for the Sick*, and the *Preces Privatae* present Andrewes in three of the traditional roles of the clergyman: as teacher, as minister to the sick, and as a master of the art of devotion.

Andrewes's *Pattern of Catechistical Doctrine* is a series of lectures on the Ten Commandments which he delivered on Saturday and Sunday afternoons when he was catechist at Pembroke College, and which proved so popular that a seventeenth-century editor called them "a very Library to young Divines."[30] The work exists in several editions, some more complete than others. Even during Andrewes's lifetime an unauthorized version was apparently in circulation, but it has not survived; an abridged edition was published in 1630 and a more complete edition in 1641. This last version was reprinted in the nineteenth-century edition of Andrewes's complete works, and is thus most easily available to modern scholars. The lectures were also published under the title *The Morall Law Expounded* by John Jackson in 1642. Whether the work in its various editions is close to the form in which Andrewes delivered it or whether it represents only sketchy notes of his auditors is a question which cannot be satisfactorily answered.

Early in the work, Andrewes defines the word "catechism," contrasting it with "the other teaching which we call preaching . . . preaching is the dilating of one member of religion into a just treatise, catechising is a contracting of the whole sum." And he defends the practice of summarizing doctrine: "The physicians have aphorisms; the lawyers, instituta; the philosophers, isagoges; and why not divines, epitomes?" Andrewes remarks that catechism is "chiefly for children," but his own *Catechism* is obviously for a learned audience.

The long introduction is composed of a Preface and a general discussion of the Law of God. The Preface is a justification of the Christian faith in general, and the position of the Church of England in particular. Here, after defending the practice of catechising, Andrewes presents six principles underlying the Christian faith: that Man's chief good is to come to God, that the way to God is by faith, that there is a God, that God rewards good and punishes evil, that the Scriptures are the Word of God, and that the Christian religion is founded on God's word. None of the ideas presented in the Preface is original. For example, the four arguments which Andrewes presents for the existence of God are altogether traditional: arguments from a first cause, from the necessity for a higher power to control the evil nature of man, from the design of the world, and from the basic knowledge of good and evil inherent in every man.

Andrewes's discussion of scriptural interpretation provides a good insight into his role as preacher and teacher of God's Word, however. In presenting differences between the Church of England and "the Papists," Andrewes emphasizes their different methods of interpreting the Bible. He firmly rejects the idea of private interpretation of the Scriptures, and stresses that the function of interpretation belongs to the learned; but he also questions the validity of the Catholic position which accepts scriptural interpretations by the Fathers, the councils, the pope, and the Church, a skepticism with respect to the Fathers which he would later abandon. Instead, he favors allegorical interpretation over the literal, a preference which he would also reveal in his sermons. Andrewes declares that "the letter is not the word," quoting Aquinas: "in a matter of faith we must take the literal sense, for other things we may make a tropological sense."[31]

The style of the Preface is distinctive. The language is so compressed that certain passages sound like Bacon: "prayer requesteth, reading searcheth, meditation findeth, contemplation directs."[32] There are also touches of the balanced, euphuistic style which would occasionally appear in Andrewes's Elizabethan sermons: "If children can say, 'Baldpate' to Elisha, why should they not say, 'Hosanna' to Christ?"; "for as in some places of the scripture the lamb may wade, so in others the elephant may swim, and we must search both." References and quotations from classical sources also abound to a greater degree here than in Andrewes's sermons; and the range of writers quoted or referred to is extensive if commonplace: Hesiod, Pythagoras, Heraclitus, Zeno, Simonides, Herodotus; Socrates, Plato, Aristotle; Diogenes, Aeschylus, Sophocles, Euripides; Menander, Epicurus, Theocritus, Lucretius; Diodorus Siculus, Cicero, Plutarch, Seneca; Pliny, Lucian, Lactantius, and Ausonius.

Finally, the Preface is remarkable because of the richness of examples and anecdotes, such as the passages found in the section on the deaths of atheists:

> Pherecydes an Assyrian being merrily disposed at a banquet amongst his friends, bragged how long he had lived and had never done sacrifice to any god; but his end was miserable, for he was devoured of lice. . . . Julian the apostate being shot in the bowels with an arrow as he was in battle against the Persians, pulled out the arrow, and receiving the blood as it gushed out into his hand, cast it into the air crying, *Vicisti Galilaee*, "Thou hast overcome me, O thou Galilean," and so died blaspheming. Lucian going to supper abroad left his hounds fast when he went, and as he returned home having railed against God and His word, his dogs fell mad and met him and tore him in pieces. . . . Machiavel rotted in the prison of Florence, as the Italians write.[33]

In his sermons, Andrewes would rarely use anecdotes such as these.

If the Preface presents the foundation of the Christian faith, the series of lectures on the Ten Commandments which follow could be described as a handbook of Christian morality. Although all of the basic ideas are derivative, Andrewes's own practical common sense and sensitivity to human behavior are revealed in passages scattered throughout the work: "and when all other sins are beaten down and consumed to ashes, even of those ashes ariseth pride; yea we are proud that we are not proud, and so pride cometh even from humility"; "if our requests be not made aright, then they are like children's prayers, that will ask a knife to hurt them, as well as bread to feed them"; "continual prosperity in temporal things is not always a sign of God's favour, but rather the contrary." "In religion there are three usual errors; . . . when we never seek more, but, 'in this I was born, and in this will I die,' and so religion findeth us and not we it"; " 'when you cease to be better, you begin to be worse,' as they that row against the stream, if they hold still, are carried backward."

In dividing the commandments, Andrewes rejects "the papist" division, declaring, "they make one commandment of the two first, and two of the last; against the most of the fathers, and so they break their own rule; again, the tenth commandment is all but one verse, and no wise man would thrust up two laws within one period."[34] Andrewes mistakenly places the Lutherans with those Protestants who reject this method of division, apparently not realizing that Luther's *Catechism* follows the traditional Catholic ordering.

Andrewes's longest lecture is on the first commandment, "Thou shalt have no other gods before me," a discussion which extends to forty-one pages in the printed text. Since the subject of the lectures is the Ten Commandments, Andrewes appropriately constructs his first lecture on the number ten, beginning with a list of the ten qualities of God: majesty, truth, unchangeableness, will, justice, mercy, knowledge, power, ubiquity, and eternity, and then nicely balancing this list with an extensive discussion of ten qualities essential to the life of the Christian: knowledge, faith, fear, humility, hope, prayer and fasting, love, true religion, sincerity, and perseverance.

Andrewes's discussion of the second commandment, "Thou shalt not make thyself any graven image," shifts the emphasis from the individual Christian to the Christian's responsibilities in corporate worship. "The eternal substance" of worship consists of preaching, prayer, the sacraments, and discipline, the same four components which Andrewes would later discuss in a sermon of 1592, when he was vicar of Saint Giles, Cripplegate. In discussing the subject of graven images in the Church, Andrewes again reveals his differences with the Church of Rome, firmly rejecting the Roman Catholic arguments justifying the use of statues. Near Andrewes's conclusion, his advice becomes practical as he discusses the proper behavior of the congregation during the Divine Service and declares that Christians "must not slumber nor sleep" at Church. It was at this period that Andrewes had his humorous encounter with the fat alderman who slept in church.

The discussion of the third commandment, "Thou shalt not take the name of the Lord, thy God, in vain," is brief, either by design, or because the printed text is incomplete. He would later devote an entire sermon, preached in 1592 when he was vicar of Saint Giles, to this commandment. His lecture on the fourth commandment, "Remember the Sabbath Day to keep it holy," is more thorough. Here he adopts the same basic position as the Puritans, and he has even been proclaimed a forerunner of the Sabbatarian movement by a modern biographer.[35] He expresses great reverence for the day: "Days, and so likewise bread and wine, are not more holy of themselves, one than another, but because they be separated and set apart for holy uses."[36] He insists that keeping the Sabbath is not a ceremony, abrogated by Christ, but a moral law which Christians must obey. To support this position, he quotes commandments from the Bible on proper behavior on the Sabbath: no gathering of food, no buying or selling, no carrying of burdens, no harvesting, and no journeying, not even to build God's house. Such a position is literal, even extreme, and Andrewes may have modified it in his later years.

In passing from the First Table to the Second, from "piety to God" to "justice towards man," Andrewes discusses extensively Jesus' words "Love thy neighbor as thyself," a discussion which gives him the opportunity to present briefly one of his favorite themes: "The angels sang 'Glory to God and peace on earth;' and there is nothing more to be desired than concord in all good, nothing more to be shunned than discord in good."[37] Andrewes devotes almost as much attention to the fifth commandment, "Honor Thy Father and Mother," as he does to the first. He observes that "God dealing seriously with man, delighteth to knit up His speech in a short compass, and therefore in one word expresseth His command. . . . so in this commandment He maketh choice of the 'father' and 'mother' to beautify the commandment, and sweeten the duty withal."[38] Andrewes extends the meaning of the word "father" by defining it as "he that hath a care or desire to do good," and his discussion includes not only the relationship between parents and children but also between rulers and subjects, husbands and wives, masters and servants, teachers and hearers, ministers and congregations, and benefactors and receivers.

He begins his lecture on this commandment with a noble statement of the traditional justification for rule, a passage which is so eloquent that it provides a classic statement of the doctrine: "God hath not made all men alike, but hath made some partakers of His excellency, and set them in superior place; others of a meaner degree, and set them in a lower place; that mutual society might be maintained. For this He hath provided in this commandment; here He establisheth the cloth and chair of estate, having given such excellency to some that He styled them gods, Ps. lxxxii.6; to these, others of inferior rank must submit and shew their observance."[39] The theme of the subject's duty to the sovereign is one which Andrewes would frequently develop in his political sermons, but in the *Catechism* he makes qualifications to the doctrine of absolute obedience, declaring that it is not absolutely due to evil men. He devotes more attention to the responsibilities of the ruler to his subjects than he does in his sermons.

His discussion of the relationship between husbands and wives is completely traditional: "And here the wife's duty is submission; not to stand upon her own will, but to be subject to her husband; which subjection must be with acknowledgment that the man is the woman's head, I Cor. xi.3; and therefore because the senses of seeing and hearing are in the head, she must see and hear by him. Yet she must not be too much kept under; for as she was made of his head, so not of his feet, but of his side, that she might be his equal." He also admonishes the women that they "must keep at home and be good house-wives."[40]

The lecture on the sixth commandment, "Thou shalt not kill," is inclusive: "Generally, therefore, whatsoever is against the life itself, or against the good estate of our life, God hath intended to comprehend in this commandment." His discussion rejects suicide but defends capital punishment and war. Later, he would develop the theme of war as justice inflicted on others in his Ash Wednesday sermon of 1599, an admonition to the Earl of Essex's men before their embarkation for the Irish Wars.

Andrewes is likewise traditional in his discussions of the remaining commandments. In his lecture on the seventh commandment, against lust, he declares that the flesh is an enemy to chastity, and that lust is watered by corrupt company, lascivious books, and "wanton pictures, or plays and spectacles of love." His lecture on the eighth commandment discusses not only stealing but also the sins of niggardliness and avarice, and his lecture on the ninth commandment condemns bearing false witness and flattery. The tenth and last lecture on covetousness is so brief (five pages) that it seems probable that the text is incomplete.

The Pattern of Catechistical Doctrine provides a good introduction to the sermons which Andrewes would later preach. Certain themes, such as the components of worship, the importance of fasting, and the duties of the subject to the monarch, would later be expanded in Andrewes's sermons, although the compacted style of his Catechism as well as the basic catechistical method of making a statement, raising objections, and then answering these objections are matters of style which would also frequently characterize his preaching. Above all, the Catechism's clarity, thorough development, careful organization, and richness of quotation are the very qualities which bring distinction to Andrewes's sermons. *The Pattern of Catechistical Doctrine* is therefore an important work of apprenticeship.

III The Manual for the Sick *and Consecration Services*

When as vicar of Saint Giles Andrewes was engaged in the very practical ministry of visiting the sick, he probably used his own *Manual of Directions for the Sick*. This work is a collection of scriptural meditations and devotions for the use of the minister in his visitations. The first complete edition was edited in 1648, twenty-two years after Andrewes's death, by Richard Drake, who also translated and edited Andrewes's *Preces Privatae* in the same year. Drake brought out his edition because he was displeased with the "many literal imperfections, omissions and misquotations"[41] of an earlier edition which has not survived.

Drake's preface "To the Christian Reader" provides an appropriate introduction to Andrewes's *Manual*, his opening sentence capturing the spirit and direction of the whole work; "The great errand of our coming into this world is but to prepare ourselves for a better." He reminds the reader "that all the business of a parish priest is not confined to the pulpit," and he emphasizes Andrewes's own sense of responsibility for his calling by quoting extensively from his sermons, concisely catching the high seriousness of Andrewes's work by citing one of his sentences: "It is not good trying conclusions about our souls." He also makes an appropriate comment about the quality of the *Manual*, "which though it speak in special to the sick, will be found upon serious thoughts, to be serviceable to all estates and conditions whatsoever, whether in sickness or health, prosperity or adversity."[42]

The *Manual* is composed of many of those passages of Scripture appropriate for the sick Christian in the various stages of his spiritual enlightenment, but, unlike Andrewes's other works, there appear to be no quotations from the Church Fathers. The numerous scriptural passages are interspersed with probing questions from the minister and recommended responses for the sick Christian. The *Manual* thus combines the devotional spirit of Andrewes's *Preces Privatae* with the method of his *Catechism.* It is designed mostly for Christians who are grievously sick or dying; and the sense of human mortality which hovers over the entire work is nicely captured in the first sentence, an ominous scriptural command: "Set thine house in order, for thou shalt die."

The *Manual* reveals the same sense of organization that is seen in all of Andrewes's works. It proceeds in an orderly fashion, following the sick Christian through various stages of his spiritual development from his acceptance of God's providence and love in sending the sickness, through contrition, repentance, and forgiveness, to litanies for the dying Christian and commendations of his soul to God. There are even scriptural passages to be delivered to the friends of the Christian after he has died.

The practical nature of the work is revealed early in a series of questions to be asked by the minister about the sick party. These questions reveal an almost clinical concern for the patient, and it is obvious that the minister is to base his strategy on the results derived from these questions:

1. Sex
2. Age
3. Condition of life.

Whether {
1. Learned, instructed?
2. Sound in Mind? / Memory?
3. The sense of hearing perfect?

Whether {
1. Patient, or unquiet?
2. Cheerful, or deject?

If being well he found comfort

In { Hearing,
Reading
Repeating particulars.

Whether any material point, whereof to be admonished?
To take occasion out of his own words.[43]

Before the minister brings any words of comfort to the sick, the fact of death is accepted in a series of "General Considerations of the Mortality of Man": "What man is he that liveth, and shall not see death? Psalm lxxxix:48. It is appointed to men once to die. Hebrews ix:27. Here we have no continuing city. Hebrews xiii:14. The night cometh, when no man can work. John ix:4." Then, after words of comfort from numerous passages of Scripture, the minister proceeds to a series of "Propositions and Inferences" designed to persuade the Christian to accept his sickness as a sign of God's favor and love:

1. You are persuaded that no sickness or cross cometh by chance to any.
2. But you believe, that it is God who sendeth them, without whose Providence they fall not on us.
3. You acknowledge God to be most wise, and to suffer nothing to befal us, but when it is expedient it so should.
4. Therefore, God having sent this His visitation to you at this time, that it is expedient for you thus to be sick. (p. 181)

The minister next asks probing questions of the sick, which will lead to contrition and repentance:

Do you acknowledge yourself not to have lived so well as you ought? But to have sinned, done amiss, and dealt wickedly?

Do you call to mind the years of your life spent amiss in the bitterness of your soul?

Do you desire to have your mind illuminated by God, touching those sins you never knew; or which you once knew, but have now forgotten: that you may repent of them? (p.183)

In such questions concerning the belief of the sick, the minister appears to be ready for any possible eventuality: "If your sense fail you, or if the pain of your disease, or weakness otherwise, so work with you, as it shall happen you with your tongue to speak aught otherwise than this your faith or religion would; Do you renounce all such words as none of yours? and is it your will we account of them as not spoken by you?" (p. 185).

There follows a series of questions designed to allow the sick party the opportunity to forgive those who have offended him and to seek forgiveness from those whom he has offended. Nor does the minister ignore the practical topic of restitution:

> Inasmuch as the offences against the Seventh Commandment, of getting any children by the act of adultery committed with the wife of another man; and against the Eighth Commandment, touching men's credits or good names, are not by God forgiven, unless restitution be made to the parties wronged; Are you ready and willing to restore and make satisfaction to such as you have wronged, in thrusting in a child begotten by you, likely to deprive the true children of the party, and begotten by him, of a child's part and portion? And, to such as you have wronged in their goods? And, to satisfy those whom you have any way touched in their good name? And that without all fraud or delay?
>
> Can you call to mind any person in particular, whom you have so offended? (pp. 186–87)

Then, after a long series of prayers from the Psalter, a significant transition occurs in which the minister for the first time identifies himself with the sick party, a union which is prepared for in the following very human prayer:

> O Lord, it is a great presumption, that one sinner should dare to commend another to thy Divine Majesty; especially, the greater, the less; and, who would not fear to undertake it? But Thy commandment it is, by Thy holy Apostle, *When any is sick, that the Priests should be called for*; that they should pray for the sick party, and that their prayers Thou wilt receive; and save and forgive the sins of the party so prayed for.
>
> And now behold, O Lord, we that are no way meet, but unworthy, utterly unworthy, to sue for ought for ourselves, charity and compassion so binding us, are enforced to become suitors to Thee for others. (p.200)

From this point on, the union of the minister with the sick Christian is emphasized by the abandonment of questions and by the substitution of the first-person plural for the second-person singular form of address.

Not only does the *Manual* exhibit Andrewes's sense of structure, but it also reveals his ability to compress great themes into small spaces, a characateristic he abundantly displays in his *Devotions* and his sermons. The acts of the Trinity are encompassed in a brief litany, and the "great merits of Jesus Christ" are compressed into the small space of six brief lines:

By His {
Agony and bloody Sweat;
Strong Crying and Tears;
Bitter Cross and Passion;
Mighty Resurrection;
Glorious Ascension;
Effectual and most acceptable Intercession and Meditation.
(p. 201)

And the notable deliverances of Old Testament heroes are compressed into seven lines, interspersed with the repeated litany for the dying Christian:

As Thou didst deliver
Noah from the flood;
    So save and deliver him.
Lot from the fire of Sodom;
    So save and deliver him.
Isaac from present death;
    So save and deliver him.
Job from all his temptations;
    So save and deliver him.
Moses from the hand of Pharaoh;
    So save and deliver him.
Daniel from the lions' den;
    So save and deliver him.
Jonas from the belly of the whale;
    So save and deliver him. (p. 202)

The *Manual for the Sick* provides a valuable supplement to Andrewes's sermons and to his life. His editor, Richard Drake, declares in his preface that Andrewes taught Christians the way to Heaven, not only "by his incomparable Sermons" but also "by his Example and Devotions."[44] Behind the keen analysis of human needs, the probing questions, and the compassion and sensitivity of the numerous prayers, we find in the *Manual* both the ideal of the seventeenth-century parson and a vivid picture of Lancelot Andrewes himself.

Services also survive which Andrewes created in his later years when he was engaged in the traditional function of visiting the churches of his bishoprics. As Bishop of Ely, he took part in the service of consecration of the Communion plate at Worcester Cathedral; and the form of service which he created for this occasion has since survived as a model for the English Church.[45] The service begins with a presentation and a prayer of offering delivered by the bishop. Then each piece of plate is presented (paten, chalices, flagons, basin, candlesticks, and censer), accompanied by appropriate passages from the Psalms and Canticles read alternately by two chaplains. The service closes with a prayer of dedication and benediction delivered by the bishop and followed by the Sacrament of Holy Communion.

As Bishop of Winchester, Andrewes created the *Form of Consecration of Church and Churchyard* for the dedication, on September 20, 1620, of Saint Mary's Extra, near Southampton. Andrewes was assisted in the service by two chaplains: Matthew and Christopher Wren.[46] The service begins with a presentation of the new church in the name of the founder, Richard Smith, followed by an alternate reading of the twenty-fourth Psalm by the chaplains. After a long prayer of dedication delivered by the bishop, the participants begin the perambulation of the church; and brief prayers are delivered at the baptistry, pulpit, reading desk, communion table, the place for marriages, and the place for burial services, concluding with an overall prayer of dedication. At this point, the congregation is admitted to the church, and various services are conducted during the remainder of the day. In the evening, the consecration of the churchyard is held. The whole service is long, beginning at eight o'clock in the morning and concluding in the evening. The form of this service, which Andrewes created, has also become a model for the English Church.

The prayers, which form the major part of the service, are quite impressive. Each prayer is appropriate for its place of delivery; and the unusually long prayer of dedication delivered before the beginning of the perambulation, with its numerous biblical echoes and its long biblical survey of hallowed places, is probably the most magnificent prayer Andrewes ever created. Especially impressive is the following expansive sentence, proclaiming the temporal and the eternal:

And whereas both in the Old and New Testament Thou has consecrated the measuring out and building of a material church to such an excellent mystery, that in it is signified and presented the fruition of the joy of Thy heavenly kingdom, we beseech Thee that in this material temple made with hands we may so serve and please Thee in all holy excercises of godliness and christian religion, that in the end we may come to that Thy temple on high, even to the holy places made without hands, whose builder and maker is God; so as when we shall cease to pray to Thee on earth, we may with all those that have in the like manner erected such places to Thy name, and with all Thy saints eternally praise Thee in the highest heavens, for all Thy goodness vouchsafed us for a time here on earth, and laid up for us there in Thy kingdom for ever and ever.[47]

The whole prayer provides an excellent model of a public prayer, just as the prayers in Andrewes's *Preces Privatae* are perfect examaples of the prayers of private devotion.

IV *The* Preces Privatae

In the greatest age of English devotional literature Andrewes's *Devotions* (*Preces Privatae*) rank high; and they remain his most appealing work. It was in such solitary times of prayer, as well as in his hours of private study, that he received the inspiration for his sermons. Andrewes frequently emphasizes the importance of the devotional life, most concisely defining the quality of devotion in his Gunpowder Day Sermon, preached in 1617: "devotion is the proper and most kindly work of holiness and in that we serve God if ever we serve Him."[48] Buckeridge called Andrewes's life a life of prayer, revealing that he spent almost five hours each day in meditation;[49] and it is in Andrewes's *Private Devotions* that his personal devotional life is most brilliantly revealed.

The *Preces Privatae* consists of a series of prayers and meditations in Greek and Latin and a few in Hebrew, these languages representing (as a modern editor has observed) the three languages of the Cross.[50] The intensity of Andrewes's devotional life is revealed by Richard Drake, who notes of one of Andrewes's holographs, "Had you seen the original manuscript, happy in the glorious deformity thereof, being slubbered with his pious hands and watered with his penitential tears, you would have been forced to confess, that book belonged to no other than pure and primitive devotion."[51] This holograph has not survived, but the work does exist in three manuscripts which provided the basis for later printed editions. The

Laudian Manuscript, not rediscovered until 1883, was apparently given by Andrewes to his friend Bishop William Laud, judging from an inscription in the manuscript.[52] Also important are the Pembroke College Manuscript in the hand of Samuel Wright, Andrewes's secretary, and the Harleian Manuscript 6614, now in the British Library, London.

The popularity of Andrewes's *Devotions* thoughout the seventeenth century is indicated by the many published editions. An incomplete version of the Greek and Latin prayers appeared in 1668 and a comprehensive edition in 1675, edited by Doctor John Lamphire. An English translation of portions of the *Devotions* was published as early as 1630 by Henry Isaacson, who had been Andrewes's secretary, and another English version of fragments appeared in 1647. This version so dissatisfied Drake that he made his own translation, published in 1648. English versions also appeared in 1655, 1670, 1674, 1682, and 1692.

The eighteenth century saw an English translation, or paraphrase (1730), by Doctor George Stanhope, the Dean of Canterbury, but it was the nineteenth century which revealed renewed interest in the work. An edition of the Latin and Greek prayers edited by James Bliss appeared in 1853 as part of the complete edition of Andrewes's works. In addition there were English translations, in 1830 by Peter Hall, and in 1839 by Edward Bickersteth, Rector of Walton. The most famous translation is that of John Henry Newman, published as the seventy-eighth of the *Tracts for the Times* (1840). This translation of Andrewes's Greek prayers was completed, in 1844, by John Mason Neale's translation of the Latin prayers. These translations were in turn revised in 1883 by Edmund Venables, Precentor of Lincoln; another edition, edited by J. E. Kempe, appeared in 1897; and an English translation of the Laudian Manuscript was edited in 1899 by P. G. Medd. An English version, edited in 1896 by the Scottish preacher Alexander Whyte, is interesting because of the pungent comments on Andrewes's life and sermons in the introduction.

The most valuable of all editions for the student of Andrewes's work, however, is the translation by F. E. Brightman, published in 1903. Not only does this work provide a complete edition of the various versions of the *Preces*, but it also presents in a logical order the prayers and meditations in a translation which is so fine that it is a work of art in itself. It was the introduction to this edition that T. S. Eliot quoted in his famous essay on Andrewes. All of the comments on Andrewes's *Devotions* which follow are also based on this edition.

Like Andrewes's sermons, his *Devotions* are carefully structured. The work begins with a basic question, "What shall I do that I may inherit eternal life?" and proceeds with a brief catechism on the Christian faith and a discussion of meditations before prayer, circumstances of prayer, and schemes of prayer. The bulk of the work is composed of morning and evening prayers, prefaced by a prose-poem. Three forms of morning prayers are presented, followed by daily morning prayers for a week, from Sunday through Saturday. Then a section of short meditations introduces the evening prayers, which are likewise presented in three different forms. The last main division is heterogeneous, consisting of a section of devotions on the Holy Mysteries of the Church: Penitence (the longest section), Confessions of Faith (Meditations on the Creed), Hope, and Charity; a series of meditations on Praise, Blessing, and Thanksgiving; and a long Deprecation, Comprecation, and Intercession. The work closes, appropriately, with devotional meditations on the Lord's Prayer.

Andrewes's *Devotions* could be called a spiritual commonplace book. Almost everything has been borrowed. As in the sermons, his chief source of quotations is the Bible, followed by the Church Fathers. He also quotes pagan writers, although to a lesser extent than in his sermons. For example, in discussing the importance of evening meditation, he cites Cato and quotes Pythagoras from Ausonius:

> Or thou compose thine eyes to slumber sweet,
> of each day's acts review the tale complete.[53]

Most surprisingly, in one of his deprecations he even quotes from the Aristophanes comedy *Plutus*, praying to be delivered "from a life unlivable" (p. 244).

Andrewes also makes abundant use of the great medieval devotional literature: Greek Service-books; the *Horologion*; Latin Service-books, including the Latin Missal; Books of Hours; the Golden Litany; the *Golden Legend* of Jacobus de Voragine; and Jewish prayers of the Synagogue. Andrewes's work thus provides a treasury of the greatest devotional literature of the past, selected, blended, and paraphrased by his sensitive mind for practical use in his own devotional life.

As in his sermons, Andrewes is highly skillful in weaving borrowed quotations into the fabric of his own work. For instance, he constructs a brief prayer of five lines, "Grace Before Meat," quoted from five different passages of Scripture, yet the five quotations are so seamlessly woven together that the prayer becomes an independent creation:

> Thou that givest food to all flesh,
> which feedest the young ravens that cry unto Thee
> And hast nourished us from our youth up:
> fill our hearts with food and gladness
> and establish our heart with thy grace. (p. 260)[54]

The morning and evening prayers reveal all the characteristics of Andrewes's devotional writing most vividly. These prayers are introduced by a comprehensive prose-poem entitled "The Dial," which traces the progress of prayer through the various hours of the day. Each stanza begins with a proclamation of a great act of God, proceeds with an application to the Christian soul, and concludes with a petition. The following stanza is illustrative:

> Thou who at eventide didst will to be taken down from the cross and buried in the tomb:
> take away our sins from us and bury them in thy sepulchre,
> covering with good works whatsoever we have committed ill,
> and save us. (p. 20)

The morning prayers for a week are effectively structured. The typical pattern, after brief introductory rubrics from the Psalms, consists of a ten-fold division: Commemoration, Penitence, Deprecation, Comprecation, Faith, Hope, Intercession, Blessing, Commendation, and Praise. Each day commemorates a day of Creation: Sunday: Light; Monday: the Firmament; Tuesday: Water and Land; Wednesday: the Sun and Moon; Thursday: Creatures of Water and Air; Friday: Creatures of Land and Man; and Saturday: the Day of Rest. Toward the end of the week, the devotions reach a climax as the theme of each day is elaborately developed in passages describing various events. The devotion for Thursday, for example, commemorates the creation of flying creatures, Christ's ascension, and the institution of the Sacrament of the Eucharist. Since Andrewes's birthday also fell on Thursday, the devotion for this day provides an interesting blending of the universal and the personal:

> By the awful mystery of the holy body and precious blood
> in the evening of this day:
> By the birthday
> of thy humble servant:
> Lord, have mercy. (p. 81)

The Daily Prayer for Friday celebrates the creation of animals and Man, the fall of Man, the promise of the redeeming seed, and the fulfillment of Redemption through the suffering of Christ on the Cross. The Daily Prayer for Saturday commemorates God's Day of Rest, associates rest with death, and concludes the entire group with the magnificent beatific vision of final rest from the Book of Revelation:

> Alleluia,
> for the Lord God omnipotent reigneth:
> let us be glad and rejoice
> and give honour to Him.
> Behold the tabernacle of God is with men
> and He will dwell with them,
> and they shall be his people
> and God himself shall be with them,
> and He shall wipe away all tears
> from their eyes,
> and there shall be no more death
> nor crying
> neither shall there be any more pain,
> for the former things
> are passed away (p. 103)

The power of the *Devotions* is displayed in their wide range of vision. "The universe hath been summed up in thy Word," Andrewes declares, in one of his morning prayers; and in the course of the prayers and meditations his imagination expands throughout the universe, soaring from the grain of mustard seed to the Heavenly Kingdom of God. His prayers also range through the life of Man, from "the sweeting of the world in infants" to "the evening of life . . . old age," "our last and closing gasp," and "the long sleep, the sleep of death, the bed of the grave, the mattrass of worms, the coverlet of dust." And at times his chains of petitions descend the great social chain of being, from the king through courtiers, Parliament, judges, and the "Christ-loving army," down to the lower orders of society for whom he offers his petitions:

> to husbandmen and graziers, good seasons;
> to the fleet and fishermen, fair weather;
> to tradesmen, not to overreach one another;
> to mechanics, to work lawfully at their occupation;
> even down to the sordid craftsmen,
> even down to the beggars. (p. 50)

The *Devotions* also achieve richness by their compression, the same quality which gives power to so many passages in Andrewes's sermons. He pays tribute to such brevity in his Nativity sermon on "little Bethlehem," declaring that the Lord finds worth in small things: "God seems to take delight . . . to bring *maxima de minimis*; great out of little.' "[55] And many passages in his *Devotions* almost appear to be invitations to the reader "to bring *maxima de minimis*," to derive great things from little passages.

At times, events are compressed to their barest essentials, as in the following description tracing Christ's first and second comings through a vertical chain of single words:

> conception
> birth
> sufferings
> cross
> death
>   burial:
> descent
> resurrection
> ascension
> session
> return
>   judgement. (p. 67)

Passages on the "mournful spectacle" of Christ's Passion in the *Devotions* reveal the same intensity found in Andrewes's Passion sermons, their very compactness contributing to their vividness, as in the following litany for Friday:

> By the sweat bloody, in clots,
>   the soul in agony,

the head wreathed with thorns driven in with the rods,
the eyes filled with tears,
the ears full of opprobries,
the mouth given to drink of vinegar and gall,
the face shamefully befouled with spitting,
the neck loaded with the burden of the cross,
the back ploughed with the weals and gashes of whips,
the hands and feet digged through,
the strong crying Eli Eli,
the heart pierced with a spear,
the water and blood flowing forth,
 the body broken,
 the blood outpoured. (p. 90)

And the accumulation of abbreviated phrases from sermons attributed to Saint Cyril, in one of Andrewes's prayers of penitence, provides an unusually powerful vision of judgment:

For then shall be a judge incorruptible,
 the judgement-seat appalling,
 the defence excuseless,
 the charges inevitable,
 the punishment summary,
 the gehenna unending,
 the angels pitiless,
 the hell enlarging her mouth,
 the river of fire sweeping on,
  of fire unquenchable,
 the prison murky,
 the darkness without ray,
 the beds of live coals,
 the worm sleepless,
 the bonds indissoluble,
 the chaos unmeasurable,
 the wall impassable,
 the weeping inconsolable;
 none { standing by,
 pleading my cause,
 plucking me forth. } (p. 166)

Andrewes' even compresses his own life into short passages scattered throughout the *Devotions*, as in the following miniature autobiography, derived from a chain of Thanksgivings. Here Andrewes praises God for:

the city,
  the church wherein I was baptised,
  the two schools
  the university,
  the college;
the parish whereof I was put in charge,
    three churches
      Southwell,
      S. Paul's
      Westminster;
    three dioceses
      Chichester,
      Ely,
      Winchester. (p. 223)

Andrewes's *Devotions*, in fact, are quite personal, showing, as his sermons do not, brief glimpses of autobiography. He prays for his parents, teachers, colleagues, and retainers; he asks to be spared from "the evils of this disease wherewith I struggle"; and he prays for the very qualities which he sought and found in his own life: "good repute," "sufficiency," "safety," "liberty," "quiet," "gravity," "purity," "ingenuity," "cheerfulness," "security," "freedom," and "tranquillity."

It is in his *Devotions* that some of Andrewes's most cherished hopes and beliefs are seen. He shows his anxiety for the Church as he prays for its deliverance:

from evils and troubles . . .
  private interpretation,
  innovation touching the sacred things
  the teaching of a different doctrine,
  doting about questions and making endless strifes,
  from heresies, schisms, scandals public, private. (p. 243)

He expresses his hopes for the English Church, which he had defended so faithfully in his works of controversy, petitioning for

the restoration of the things that are wanting }
the strengthening of the things that remain } therein. (p. 60)

And he appears to suggest, in a portion of his prayer for grace, a most personal desire for his own life:

Grant me the power and the opportunity of welldoing,
  that before the day of my decease
    I may at all adventure effect some good thing,
      whereof the fruit may remain. (p. 254)

A large proportion of the *Devotions* is penitential, and one of Andrewes's editors, Alexander Whyte, has suggested that this emphasis betrays Andrewes's sensitivity to the sins and compromises of his public life: "But as David's heart came back to him from adultery and murder in the Fifty-first Psalm, so did Bishop Andrewes's heart come back to him from servility and sychophancy and the sale of justice in many a confession and in many a commendation of his *Private Devotions*."[56] Such an extreme position, however, appears to ignore the fact that contrition is the essential foundation for the devotional life of any Christian saint; and it is unfair to hold Andrewes's penitential prayers as factual evidence of a sinful life.[57]

Occasionally the *Devotions* reveal attitudes not found in the sermons. For example, Andrewes almost never refers to Christ's mother in his sermons, but in one passage of the *Devotions* he pays her the greatest reverence in commemorating "the allholy, immaculate, more than blessed mother of God and evervirgin Mary" (p. 85). By and large, however, the *Devotions* and the sermons are closely related in spirit. This relationship has been most concisely noted by the editor F. E. Brightman: "The devotions are in fact an abstract of the sermons, the sermons a development and expansion of the devotions. The things which he delivers to the Church are the things in which he habitually 'exercises himself day and night'; they have been proved and tested in his own heart; and the essence of his public teaching is distilled into suggestion for his own devotion."[58]

The *Devotions* repeatedly demonstrate Andrewes's sensitivity to the great responsibilities borne by the preacher of God's Word. One prayer expresses his consciousness of the exaltedness of his calling: "O Thou coal of double nature, which in the tongs didst touch the lips of the prophet and take away his iniquity: touch my lips, who am a sinner, and purge me of every stain and make me skill to shew forth thine oracles" (p. 258). Another prayer delivered before preaching and based on Christ's commission to his disciples, "I will make you fishers of men," effectively compresses the preacher's responsibility into a series of simple analogies:

World	Sea	
Men	Fishes	
Church	Boat	
Preacher	Fisher	
Word	Net	(p. 257)

And it is possible that before Andrewes went up to the pulpit, he kept in mind the following admonition from Fulgentius:

Let the preacher labour to be heard gladly, intelligently, obediently. And let him not question that he can do this better by the piety of his prayers than by the fluency of his speech. By praying for himself and for them he is going to address, let him be a bedesman or ever he be a teacher: and approaching devoutly, before he put forth a speaking tongue, let him lift up to God a thirsty soul, that so he may give out what from Him he hath drunk in, and empty out what he hath first replenished. (p. 257)

This prayer aptly indicates how closely Andrewes's devotional life was intertwined with his preaching, his private and public writing in total, harmonious concord.

CHAPTER 3

Lancelot Andrewes as Preacher

ANDREWES'S greatest reputation was won in the pulpit, as court preacher to Queen Elizabeth and King James. In the most glorious period of the English sermon, he was honored by his contemporaries as *Stella Praedicantium* and proclaimed "an angel in the pulpit."[1]

The popularity of sermons in Andrewes's time may be determined from contemporary records of the large number of people who flocked to hear them and of the numerous sermons which poured from the presses. Andrewes himself was aware of their popularity, and he declares in his Ash Wednesday sermon preached in 1623: "A wonderful thing it is how many sermons, and sermons upon sermons, as it were so many measures of seed, are thrown in daily, and what becomes of them no man can tell."[2] And he must have observed the behavior of congregations while attending sermons, since he vividly comments on their casual attitude in his Gunpowder Day sermon preached in 1617: "We come to it if we will, we go our ways when we will; stay no longer than we will, and listen to it while we will; and sleep out, or turn us and talk out, or sit still and let our minds rove the rest whither they will; take stitch at a phrase or word, and censure it how we will. So the word serves us to make us sport; we serve not it."[3]

I *Andrewes's Attitude to the Sermon*

Andrewes's own attitude to his calling and to the function of the sermon may be determined from comments scattered throughout his sermons. It is important to realize that for Andrewes, as for other members of the Church of England, the sermon constituted only a portion of the divine service, which also contained prayer and participation in the Sacrament of the Eucharist. Not only was Andrewes well aware of the immense popularity of sermons in his time, but he was also concerned with the congregation's enthusiasm for preaching, often at the expense of other parts of the service. He expresses his concern in the same sermon in which he comments on the behavior of congregations: "The word [sermon] is holy, I know, and I wish it all the honour that may be; but God forbid we should think that *in hoc uno sunt omnia*. All our 'holiness' is in hearing, all our service ear-service; that were in effect as much as to say all the body were an ear."[4] In an early sermon, preached before King James in 1607, Andrewes comments on the popularity of preaching and laments the absence of members of the congregation at other parts of the service: "now is the world of sermons. For proof whereof, as if all godliness were in hearing of sermons, take this very place, the house of God, which now you see meetly well-replenished; come at any other parts of the service of God (parts, I say, of the service of God no less than this) you shall find it in a manner desolate."[5]

Andrewes recognized that the popularity of sermons frequently was owing to their style rather than their content, and at times he emphasizes to the congregation the importance of the preacher's message. Thus he warns in the 1607 sermon, "The music of a song, and the rhetoric of a sermon, all is one. A foul error, even in the very nature of the word; for that is a law, a testament and neither song nor sonnet."[6] In his Pentecost sermons, Andrewes frequently discusses preaching, and in a sermon preached in 1608 he attacks flashy preaching devoid of substance: "sure it is that volubility of utterance, earnestness of action, straining the voice in a passionate delivery, phrases and figures, these all have their heat, but they be but blazes. It is the evidence of the Spirit in the soundness of the sense, that leaves the true impression. . . . The rest come in passion; move for the present, make us a little sermon-warm for the while; but after they flit and vanish, and go their way—true mark leave they none."[7] Yet in the same sermon he emphasizes the exaltedness of preaching, comparing it to the sending of the Holy Ghost at Pentecost, defining preaching as "the taking of the spirit of the preacher, and putting it on the hearer; or to express it by the type of fire, the lighting of one torch by another, that so it might pass from man to man, till all were lightened."[8] Near the end of his preaching career he concisely states the purpose of the sermon: "The only true praise of a sermon is, some evil left, or some good done upon the hearing of it."[9] But Andrewes's simplest statement on the preacher's responsibilities occurs in his *Catechism*, delivered when he was a young man to the students of Cambridge: "the minister must deliver the word . . . with authority, gravity, and majesty; as knowing that it is not his own word, but the everlasting truth of God."[10]

Although Andrewes frequently emphasizes the significance of the content of the preacher's message, he never denies the importance of an appropriate style. In his *Catechism* he declares that the minister "must not only have 'old matters,' but, 'new:' not new doctrine, but new ways of expressing."[11] And he certainly must have realized the importance of conveying the message as effectively as possible in a style which would be pleasing to his select, sophisticated court congregation, an audience in which sat a king who considered himself not only a scholar and theologian but also a man of literary abilities. It is Andrewes's sermons, however, which best display his enthusiasm for style, and they certainly reveal all three of the traditional goals of the preacher which Augustine had enunciated Christianizing Horace: to teach, to move, to delight.

II *Influences on Andrewes's Sermons*

Andrewes's sermons are enriched by three sources: the Bible, classical literature, and the Church Fathers. The Bible is the most important source, providing those texts which become the framework for his sermons, the majority of which are developments or analyses of scriptural passages. His characteristic method is conveniently described by an anonymous seventeenth-century commentator, who declares that Andrewes "dives to the very bottom of the text, and fetches out all the bowels of it."[12] Andrewes himself, in his Pentecost sermon preached in 1617, comments favorably on the traditional method of constructing a sermon by close biblical exegesis. In discussing Christ's first sermon he declares that "He took a text, to teach us thereby to do the like. To keep us within; not to fly out, or preach much, neither without, or besides the book."[13]

In interpreting the Bible to the congregation, Andrewes is aware of the traditional fourfold interpretation of Scripture. His most extensive discussion of this subject occurs at the beginning of his Pentecost sermon preached in 1614, where, in presenting the text, "Thou art gone up on high," he discusses in ascending order the four different senses of the text: the literal (Moses' ascending Sinai), the analogical (David's going up to Mount Sion), the moral (the exaltation of God's people, whenever they are "made thrall to their enemies"), and the prophetical (Christ's ascension into Heaven).[14] This sermon ignores the literal sense and develops only the prophetical sense—a method which Andrewes frequently follows—since this level of meaning provides him with the richest possibilities for developing a text. And this practice is not exceptional. In his Resurrection sermon, for instance, preached in 1612 on the text "Purge out therefore the old leaven," he asks at the beginning of the sermon, "What is the spirit of this letter?"[15] And in his Resurrection sermon preached in 1623 on the powerful text from Isaiah "Who is this that cometh from Edom, with red garments?" he declares, echoing Saint Paul, "Go we then to the kernel and let the husk lie; let go the dead letter, and take we to us the spiritual meaning that hath some life in it."[16] But in his attack on the Pharisees, in his Resurrection sermon delivered in 1617, he is satisfied with the literal meaning of the words "adulterous generation," declaring, "For my part I see no harm to take the word in the native sense without figure, for men given to commit that sin, the sin of adultery."[17]

For the modern reader whose knowledge of the Bible is limited, it is interesting to observe the facility with which Andrewes's imagination ranges over the Scriptures, embellishing his development of the sermon text with numerous quotations from other biblical passages. At times, his paragraphs are illuminated by the density of scriptural references, as in the following passage from his Pentecost sermon preached in 1617 in which he develops the idea "No respect of persons with God" by alluding to various examples from the New Testament: "The tidings of the Gospel are as well for 'Lydia the purple seller' as for 'Simon the tanner;' for 'the Areopagite,' the judge at Athens, as for 'the jailor' at Philippi; for 'the elect lady' as for widow 'Dorcas;' for the 'Lord Treasurer of Ethiopia' as for the beggar at the beautiful gate of the temple;' for 'the household of Caesar' as for 'the household of Stephanas;' yea and, if he will, for 'king Agrippa' too."[18]

Quotations from classical literature also embellish Andrewes's sermons. Some Puritans of his age had objected to the practice of preachers using quotations from heathen writers in their sermons, but Andrewes, in an early sermon delivered in 1592, lists this objection as a "vain imagination," defends the practice by reminding the congregation that Saint Paul himself had quoted the heathen, and declares that "it is not unlawful neither to reason from the wisest and most pithy sayings of natural men."[19] And near the end of his preaching career, in his first Wise Men sermon delivered in 1620, Andrewes makes an eloquent defense of classical learning: "there is no truth at all in human learning or philosophy that thwarteth any truth in Divinity, but sorteth well with it and serveth it, and all to honour Him Who saith of Himself *Ego sum Veritas*, 'I am the Truth' "[20]

The range of Andrewes's borrowings from the classical tradition is also extensive. His Lenten sermons alone contain quotations from Pliny, Herodotus, Seneca, Aeschylus, Livy, Aristotle, Juvenal, Terence, and Petronius. He has the ability to work borrowed material naturally into his own work. For example, in his Ash Wednesday sermon preached before Queen Elizabeth in 1589 on the text "When He slew them, then they sought Him" (Psalm 78:34), he freely paraphrases one of the speeches of the Messenger in Aeschylus' *Persians* as a vivid example of how even professed atheists seek God when they face death: "when the Grecian forces hotly pursued our hosts, and we must needs venture over the great water Strymon, frozen then but beginning to thaw, when an hundred to one we had all died for it—that is, *cum occideret*, with mine eyes I saw saith he . . . Of those gallants whom I had heard before so boldly maintain there was no God to seek . . . 'then every one of them on their knees and full devoutly praying the ice might hold till they got over.' "[21] Extensive quotations such as this are rare; it is more characteristic forAndrewes briefly to quote or allude to a classical source, most often without mentioning the author. Occasionally the modern reader is surprised at an unexpected classical reference embedded in a sermon. In a passage in his 1605 Passion sermon discussing the scourging of Jesus, a brief quotation from a comedy by Terence appears as an example of the shame of the whip: "Loris? liber sum" (The Whip? I am free).[22]

A far more pervasive influence than classical sources is the tradition of the Church Fathers. In the course of his sermons, Andrewes frequently quotes from their works to support his arguments or to embellish his style. Apparently Andrewes's attitude to the Fathers underwent a change early in his preaching career. As a student at Cambridge, his *Catechism* reveals skepticism on the value of their interpretations: "For the fathers and the councils we say, if there be doubt in the scriptures, there is much more in the exposition . . . they say their exposition is true; now that must needs be meant when they agree all in one, or else which of them shall we believe? But we shall not find one place of a hundred which they all expound alike, so that few of their expositions should be received."[23]

Andrewes's attitude soon changed. Almost every page of his sermons is adorned with quotations from the Fathers in Latin, and occasionally in Greek. In discussing the anointing of the Spirit in his Pentecost sermon preached in 1617, he affirms the spiritual power of the books "of the ancient Fathers and lights of the Church, in whom the scent of this ointment was fresh, and the temper true."[24] This ointment flows through the sermons, enriching the preacher's words with the long tradition of the Christian past. For example, in discussing the importance of praise for the Christian in his Resurrection sermon preached in 1614, the paragraph is considerably enhanced by a quotation from Jerome on the quality of praise in the Primitive Church: "Their Amen . . . was like a clap of thunder, and their Allelujah as the roaring of the sea."[25]

The most significant influence of the Fathers on Andrewes's sermons, however, is on his prose style. From them as well as from his own age, he inherited his enthusiasm for parallelism and antithetical constructions, his fondness for wordplay, and his delight in farfetched metaphors. Indeed, much of Andrewes's celebrated "metaphysical" imagery is actually derived from the Fathers. The famous paradoxical metaphor of the *Verbum Infans,* the word without a word, which so frequently occurs in the Nativity sermons, was borrowed by Andrewes from Bernard. And in describing the crucifixion of Jesus, in his Passion sermon preached in 1605, he uses an extravagant metaphor, also from Bernard: "the nails and spearhead serve as keys to let us in."[26]

III *Andrewes's Prose Style*

Although Andrewes's sermons are enriched by other sources, his own prose style is quite distinctive. Especially evident is his love of words and his sensitivity to the possibilities of language, an enthusiasm which is shown in several ways. It is found in his devotion to the sermon text, and in the thoroughness with which he examines each word of the text, a characteristic which has been aptly described by T. S. Eliot: "Andrewes takes a word and derives the world from it; squeezing and squeezing the word until it yields a full juice of meaning which we should never have supposed any word to possess."[27] His enthusiasm for words is dramatically revealed in a famous passage in his Nativity sermon preached in 1614, in which he playfully dissects the word "Immanuel" into its three components, endows them with life, and, in effect, presents them as characters in a brief narrative. And he again reveals his awareness of the vitality of words in his Nativity sermon on Psalm 85, delivered in 1616, in which he takes the four words describing God—Mercy, Truth, Righteousness, and Peace—and makes them female, presenting them in passages which have the spirit of the dramatic masque.

Andrewes is sensitive to the sound of words, and his sermons are filled with wordplay, puns, and neologisms. He frequently rhymes words, as in his paraphrase of the angel's reassuring words to the frightened shepherds, "your terror groweth out of error"; and in his violent attack on hypocrites, in which he declares that they will "lie together and fry together" in Hell. He also frequently brings together in the same sentence words of similar sounds in order to emphasize differences, as in his contrast of Christ's two appearances, "He that cometh here in clouts, He will come in the clouds one day"; in his condemnation of hypocrites, "It was not their double-fast, but their double-face"; and in his brief comment on Herod, "His worshipping will prove worrying." He delights in punning, as in this description of the abasement of Christ: "He that sits on the throne thus be thrown in a manger"; in his reference to "the first day of Lent as a time lent us"; and in his question about the sign of Jonah: "What is the profit of this sign of the Prophet?" He even creates new words. In the same Nativity sermon in which he performs the word dissection, he coins the grotesque words "Immanu-hell" and "Immanu-all," and later calls Christ's death a "satis-passion." In another Nativity sermon, he speaks of Christ's being "minorated" and "minimated" when he left Heaven for earth.

Although most of the sermons were delivered to sophisticated court audiences, they contain expressions which are highly colloquial, revealing Andrewes's enthusiasm for the vitality of common language. His sermons are filled with such proverbial expressions as "to follow through thick and thin," "the saving of our skin," "the coast is clear," "to turn tail," "to play fast or loose," "to set altogether by the ears," "to touch home," "not to give over school," "not to busy our brains," "at the first blush," "at the first dash," "no slipping of the collar." Most often it is when Andrewes's emotions are aroused that he shifts to colloquial language, as in his concise denunciation of the Pharisees—"the whole bunch was no better"—and in his colorful description of their coming to Christ: "they came but by a birding, but to catch from Him some advantage . . . and laid it up for a rainy day."

Such use of proverbs becomes very common for Andrewes.[28] When he discusses mankind's alienation from Heaven before the appearance of the Angel to the shepherds, he declares, "In a troubled water no face will well be seen, nor by a troubled mind no message received, till it be settled." In alluding to the fortunate discovery of the Gunpowder Plot he asserts, "Better a good buckler to keep off the blow, than a good plaster to heal the hurt of it." And to emphasize the paradox of Christ's being born in little Bethlehem, he employs an especially homely proverb: "How huge an oak from how small an acorn."

The words which Andrewes favors are simple, mostly monosyllabic, while the sentences and phrases he prefers are aphoristic. He expresses his preference in a frequently quoted passage from his sermon on the short text "Remember Lot's Wife": "it fareth with sentences as with coins: in coins, they that in smallest compass contain greatest value are best esteemed: and in sentences those that in fewest words comprise most matter, are most praised."[29] These words could fittingly be applied to Andrewes's own sentences; and Eliot's description of him as the "master of the short sentence"[30] is certainly deserved.

Some of these short sentences are quite striking, but they are often so embedded in the paragraph that the reader may overlook their beauty. It is the sentences and phrases which, at times, convey most precisely and eloquently the preacher's thoughts. For example, in his Pentecost sermon preached in 1621, Andrewes develops in a paragraph the idea that God bestows small gifts as well as great, but he communicates his meaning most effectively in a single sentence with three nicely balanced clauses: "He That made the elephant, made the ant; He That the eagle, the fly; He That the most glorious Angel in Heaven, the poorest worm that creeps on the earth." In a Nativity sermon, he expresses the difficult concept underlying the text "And the Word was made Flesh," most beautifully in a sentence employing a familiar seventeenth-century image: "Through the veil of His flesh such beams He cast as behind those clouds they might know there was a sun." He represents the paradox of Christ's birth in a sentence which fascinated Eliot: "*Verbum infans,* the Word without a word the eternal Word not able to speak a word." And he is able to suggest the glory of God in one sentence: "There is a part of divinity that dazzles: if we look too long on it, we may well lose our sight." At times the sentences bear the wisdom of the common proverb: "Men set great titles upon empty boxes"; "Humility is the Bethlehem of virtues"; "Never trust a repentance repentine, no sudden flash or brunt." And much of the power of Andrewes's most famous sermon, the Wise Men sermon of 1622, lies in the many brilliant sentences which flash throughout the work: "The star in their hearts cast one beam out at their mouths"; "It is not commended to stand 'gazing up into Heaven' too long; not on Christ himself ascending, much less on His star"; "It was no summer progress. A cold coming they had of it"; "Christ is no wild-cat."

The short sentences and phrases which make up Andrewes's paragraphs provide a good example of the Senecan prose style favored in the early seventeenth century. This stylistic movement represented a reaction against Ciceronianism, with its long, involved, slowly compounding sentences favored earlier by Elizabethan writers. These two different styles are nicely displayed in the prose of the two great Anglican divines of the period: Hooker and Andrewes. Hooker's sermons, as well as his *Ecclesiastical Polity*, provide the best example in English of the effective use of the Ciceronian style, while Andrewes's sermons remain an excellent example of English Senecanism.

One criticism often leveled against the Senecan style is that the terseness of the sentences may cause obscurity, and jerkiness in the paragraphs. Andrewes is never obscure, but at times the extreme brevity of his sentences does give a disjointed appearance to his paragraphs, as in the following instance from his Resurrection sermon preached in 1613:

> Thus then it lieth. Christ is risen, and if Christ, then we. If we so be, then we "seek;" and that we cannot, unless we "set our minds." To "set our minds" then. On what? "On things above." Which above? Not "on earth," so is the text, but "where Christ is." And why there? Because, where He is, there are the things we seek for, and here cannot find. There "He is sitting;"—so at rest. And "at the right hand;"—so in glory. "God's right hand;"—and so for ever. These we seek, rest in eternal glory. These Christ hath found, and so shall we, if we make this our *agendum;* begin this day to "set our minds" to search after them.[31]

Extreme examples such as this are far less common than paragraphs in which the sentences coherently and powerfully develop a central idea. It is difficult to generalize, but an examination of

Andrewes's sermons reveals certain types of paragraph development. One type develops the main idea by means of reiteration, another by a series of antitheses, and still another presents an orderly development, illustrating either an expansion in space or a progression in time. Some of the paragraphs of reiteration give the impression of being needlessly repetitive, but the paragraphs which present a development in space or time are among the most impressive passages in Andrewes's sermons. (Some of these patterns of paragraph development will be discussed more specifically in later chapters on specific groups of Andrewes's sermons.) Andrewes's words are simple, his sentences are brief, and his paragraphs are, by and large, short, much shorter than those of Donne. He could appropriately be called a master of brevity.

In developing his paragraphs, Andrewes's prose is enhanced by the power and richness of his imagery. Most often, his images are suggested by his sermon texts, but his imagination ranges farther afield at times. Many of his images, such as maps, perspective glasses, and the images derived from medicine and law, are common to his age. Especially prominent in his work are images from the theater and from nature.

Andrewes has been frequently criticized for those farfetched images which have been labeled "metaphysical." His critics have apparently overlooked the fact that even the Bible, his main source of inspiration, contains such imagery: the Old Testament prophet compares Man's righteousness to "filthy rags" and his idolatry to a "menstruous cloth," while Jesus, looking ahead to his crucifixion, alludes to it as a second baptism and He compares His second coming to the appearance of a thief in the night. Much of Andrewes's "metaphysical" imagery was borrowed from the Church Fathers, not the Bible, but some of it was also apparently original. The effect of this kind of imagery is surprise, and its justification lies in its very extravagance, which indelibly impresses the point being illustrated on the minds of the congregation or reader. Who can forget the grotesquely humorous imagery in Andrewes's question on the Holy Ghost and Christ?: "Are they like two buckets? one cannot go down, unless the other go up?" or his extravagant conceit on the Jesuits and the Gunpowder Plot, which would have been for "Jesus to have blown up Christ"? Equally memorable is his famous comparison of the Gunpowder conspirators to children in the womb and to the men inside the Trojan horse.

Perhaps the aspect of Andrewes's style which is most remote to the modern reader is his practice of weaving Latin (and occasionally Greek and Hebrew) words, phrases, and sentences into the fabric of his English prose. Andrewes's court congregations were just as familiar with Latin as with English, and they probably found his practice not only acceptable but desirable. Since Andrewes almost always follows a Latin quotation with an English translation, he achieves both richness and emphasis, as in the following passage from his first Nativity sermon in which the suggestiveness of the Latin words and the repetition of the idea in English blend to create a vivid picture of the miserable abode of man: "*inter pulices, et culices, tineas, arcaneas et vermes;* our place is here 'among fleas and flies, moths and spiders, and crawling worms.' There is our place of dwelling."[32] And the Latin phrases often contribute to the effectiveness of entire paragraphs, as in a passage from one of the Nativity sermons in which the various stages of the life of Christ are suggestively presented by the Latin phrases: "*Verbum infans . . . Sudans et algens . . . Cujus livore sanati.*"[33]

Andrewes's playfulness with words is just as evident in Latin as in English: "when *spes* becomes *res,*" "where *votum* is *totum,*" "that had been *virgo decipiet,* not *concipiet.*" And he is sensitive to the potentialities of each language. In his Gunpowder Day sermon on the mercies of God preached in 1615, he realizes the superiority of the Latin word "misericordia" over the English word "mercy" and he presents a brief verbal anatomy: "It is not so plain, this, in our English word mercy, as in the Latin *misericordia,* for there is misery full out at the length."[34]

Andrewes's enthusiasm for the language of the Latin Vulgate, as well as for the English translations of the Bible, is an important element not only in his style but also in his exegetical method. He is reluctant to miss any opportunity to find as much meaning as possible in his sermon texts, as his following comment indicates: "and for my part I wish no word ever narrowed by a translation, but as much as might be left in the latitude of the original tongue."[35]

IV *Structure of Andrewes's Sermons*

With Andrewes the whole is more important than the parts. All of his sermons are carefully structured, and most of them single-mindedly and thoroughly develop the sermon text, piece by piece and word by word. His sermons are more highly structured than those of Donne, who frequently wanders away from the text, many of his most brilliant passages being digressions. Experiencing an Andrewes sermon, however, is like taking a journey in which there are few departures from the itinerary mapped out by the text. Andrewes's careful sense of structure is what Eliot called the ordonnance of his style.[36]

In constructing his sermons, Andrewes closely follows the traditional pattern inherited from the Middle Ages, a structure which is just as formal as the movement of a symphony. Although the names assigned to the sermon's parts vary, the typical sermon is divided into three main sections: the introduction or exordium (including the division of the text), the development or exposition of the text, and the conclusion. In a typical Andrewes sermon, the introduction discusses the significance of the day on which the sermon is delivered and the appropriateness of the text for the day. The division of the text, what Andrewes calls "the partition," is part of the introduction. Not only does it break down the text into divisions and subdivisions, but it also serves as a convenient outline or map for the whole sermon which is to follow. In preaching each sermon, Andrewes apparently paused for a prayer between the division and the exposition, a break which is indicated typographically in early editions of his sermons. After the introduction the exposition follows, which is usually a thorough development or analysis of the text, the main part of the sermon. Finally comes the conclusion, which is usually an application of the exposition to the congregation, although occasionally Andrewes makes applications after the divisions and subdivisions of the exposition. Although most of Andrewes's sermons could be described as thorough developments or close analyses of the texts, there are two other, less common types: the sermon which is, essentially, a lecture on a topic (Andrewes's Ash Wednesday sermon, preached in 1621 on the subject of fasting) and the sermon of memorial (his beautiful Elizabethan sermon, memorializing Lot's wife).

V *Content of Andrewes's Sermons*

Andrewes's style and method were not ends in themselves, but means by which to convey, most effectively, the message. The themes are those basic to Christianity: Man's fall and his redemption through the sacrificial death and glorious Resurrection of Jesus Christ. They are presented against the vivid background of the great holy days of the Christian church; and Andrewes celebrates the paradox of the Incarnation, the sacrifice and triumph of the Passion, the glory of the Resurrection, and the bounty of Pentecost. He also frequently reminds his congregations of their duties to God and king, but since the sermons emphasize the universal rather than the temporal, they contain few references to contemporary events and men. The Gunpowder Plot stimulated Andrewes's imagination more than any other contemporary event. He also mentions the dearth of 1594 in a Lenten sermon delivered that year; the English victory over the Spanish Armada in his Gunpowder sermons and in his Pentecost sermon preached in 1614; and the Saint Bartholomew Day's Massacre and the assassinations of the French kings Henry III and Henry IV in his Gunpowder and Gowrie Day sermons.

In emphasizing the basic themes of Christianity, Andrewes's sermons avoid controversial doctrines. Not one of his sermons contains any reference to the perplexing doctrine of predestination. His convictions on the proper themes for sermons may be determined from a passage in his Nativity sermon, preached in 1607 on the text "And without controversy great is the mystery of godliness" (I Timothy 3:16): "a false conceit is crept into the mind of men, to think points of religion that be manifest to be certain petty points, scarce worth the hearing. Those—yea those be great, and none but those, that have great disputes about them. It is not so. . . . Those that are necessary He hath made plain: those that are not plain not necessary."[37] This passage provides a valuable glimpse of Andrewes's basic attitude to his task as a preacher; and his sermons are devoted not to disputed points but to the "necessary" and "plain" truths of Christianity.

VI *Andrewes's Preaching Style*

The prose style and the content of Andrewes's sermons are evident to anyone who studies them, but is it possible to determine anything of his pulpit style or to catch glimpses of his personality in his sermons? The art of the preacher, like that of the actor, should be self-effacing, although there have been preachers, both in the past and at present, who vividly project their own personalities from the pulpit. In this respect Andrewes's sermons reveal a strikingly different pulpit style from Donne's, for Donne in his sermons projects an extremely vivid persona, as dazzling as some of the speakers in his dramatic monologues. Andrewes, however, reveals almost nothing of his personality in his sermons, except for a delightful sense of humor and a touch of modesty in his occasional embarrassment at the earthiness of some biblical texts which he refuses to translate for the congregation.

It is Eliot who has most vividly emphasized the differences between the preaching styles of the two men. His description of Donne as "the religious spellbinder, the Reverend Billy Sunday of his time, the flesh-creeper, the sorcerer of emotional orgy"[38] seems unfairly severe, but his comparison of the homiletic methods of Andrewes and Donne is perceptive: "Andrewes' emotion is purely contemplative; it is not personal, it is wholly evoked by the object of contemplation, to which it is adequate; his emotions wholly contained in and explained by its object. . . . Donne is a 'personality' in a sense in which Andrewes is not: his sermons, one feels, are a 'means of self-expression.' He is constantly finding an object which shall be adequate to his feelings; Andrewes is wholly absorbed in the object and therefore responds with the adequate emotion."[39]

Andrewes is, indeed, self-effacing; the emphasis is on the text rather than on the preacher, on the message and not the messenger. This is not to say that his sermons lack a dramatic voice but that some of his most dramatic moments occur when he is creating the speeches of others. At times he paraphrases the words of the angels ("Your terror groweth out of error") and even God Himself ("My touches and My twitches . . . shew . . . that many times I would when you would not"). One of his finest passages is the dramatic speech of Christ which concludes the famous Wise Men sermon. Andrewes is especially dramatic when he anticipates and gives voice to thoughts and objections which may lurk in the minds of his congregation, and it is these passages which most vividly display his sense of humor.

His humor reveals itself in the most unexpected places, frequently in the most serious contexts, even while he is expounding the Divine mysteries. His playfulness appears in discussing the Incarnation in his first Nativity sermon, where, in presenting the words of the text "For He in no wise took the Angels, but the seed of Abraham he took" he declares that the Angels "will take no offence at it; they will not remove Jacob's ladder for all this, or descend to us, or ascend for us, ever a whit the slower, because he is become 'the Son of Man.' "[40] He even injects humor into his discussion of the death of Jesus, in a Resurrection sermon where he pretends ironically to object to the haste of the women in rushing to Jesus' tomb:

"Why good Lord, what need all this haste? Christ is fast enough under His stone. He will not run away ye may be sure."[41] And in another Resurrection sermon, he recalls the Crucifixion as he playfully objects to Christ's strange command to Mary, "Touch Me not": "What speak we of that when not three days since He suffered other manner of touches and twitches both? Then *noli Me tangere* would have come in good time."[42] The predominant quality of this humor is irony, and his favorite objects of attack are the Pharisees and the hypocrites as well as those two extreme deviations from the Anglican *via media,* the Jesuit at the one extreme, and the "brainsick Anabaptist" at the other.

VII *The Printed Sermons*

The first collected edition of Andrewes's sermons was published by his friends John Buckeridge and William Laud at the command of King Charles I in 1629, three years after Andrewes's death.[43] Other editions followed in 1632, 1635, 1641, and 1661. According to Isaacson, Andrewes's sermons, collected in the first edition, were "but a handful of those which he preached."[44] It is not possible to determine whether the first two editors published all of Andrewes's sermons which came into their hands or if they adopted some principles of selection. All but four of the ninety-six sermons are court sermons, most of them preached to King James and his courtiers in the Royal Chapel at Whitehall. It would be interesting for the student of Andrewes's work to have more examples of the sermons preached to his parishioners when he was vicar of Saint Giles in addition to the two which survive, and it is tantalizing to imagine what kind of sermon he preached in 1589 at Deptford to the sailors who were members of Trinity House, the organization over which his father had been master. Andrewes mentions that he was to preach to this company in a letter to Sir Francis Walsingham,[45] but the sermon, if preached, has not survived. Perhaps the court sermons reveal just one facet of Andrewes the preacher, but this cannot now be known.

Andrewes took great care in preparing and revising his sermons. His editor Buckeridge relates in his funeral sermon: "Most of his solemn Sermons he was most careful of, and exact; I dare say few of them but they passed his hand, and were thrice revised, before they were preached."[46] And it is fairly certain that the texts printed by the first editors are a faithful representation of the sermons which

Andrewes actually delivered. In their comments on the first edition the editors state, "There came to our hands a world of Sermon notes, but these came perfect. Had they not come perfect, we should not have ventured to adde any limme unto them, lest mixing a pen farre inferiour, we Should have disfigured such compleat bodies . . . as the Sermons were preached, so are they published."[47]

The ninety-six sermons are divided, except for eleven miscellaneous ones, according to the great holy days of the Christian Church: there are seventeen Nativity sermons, six sermons delivered in Lent, eight Ash Wednesday sermons, three on the Passion, eighteen on the Resurrection, and fifteen on the sending of the Holy Ghost at Pentecost. There are also eight sermons celebrating King James's deliverance from the Gowrie Conspiracy (August 5) and ten preached on the anniversary of his escape from the Gunpowder Plot (November 5).[48] These days of deliverance also were regarded in England as holy days.

In the following chapters it will be most convenient first to examine the miscellaneous and Lenten sermons, most of which are early work, and then to turn to the festival sermons.

CHAPTER 4

Early Sermons

I *The Spittal Sermon*

ANDREWES'S "Sermon Preached at the Spittle" is of special interest because it is his first surviving sermon. It was preached in the yard of Saint Mary's Hospital, London, on April 10, 1588, the Wednesday morning of Easter week. The outdoors sermon was, in practice, approximately twice as long as the typical hour-length sermon preached in a church, and the "Spittal Sermon" is the longest of Andrewes's surviving sermons, extending to fifty pages in the modern text. Although the work is too long for modern tastes, it is a fine sermon, providing a good introduction to his preaching style.

The Spittal Sermon is addressed to a congregation of the chief citizens of London: lawyers, merchants, and businessmen. The text is "Charge them that are rich in this world, that they be not high-minded" (I Timothy 6:17–19), and in his introduction Andrewes notes the appropriateness of the text for his congregation, calling it "the rich man's Scripture." The whole sermon reveals Andrewes's ability to adapt his message and style to his audience. Several of his examples are appropriate to the special interests of his congregation, as is his humorously ironic comparison of the hardships of Saint Paul to the perils of the modern rich man and his vivid examples drawn from the contemporary world. This passage also illustrates Andrewes's love of parallelism and antithesis, an enthusiasm which would be especially prominent in his early sermons but which would continue throughout his whole preaching career:

And sure if the rich will glory they must glory with St. Paul, for they are in all, and in more, and greater [infirmity] than the Apostle ever was. He was "in perils of water," they in peril both of water and fire; he was "in peril of robbers," they in peril of rovers by sea, and robbers by land; he "in peril of his own nation," they are in peril of our own nation and of other nations, both removed as the Moor and Spaniard, and near home as the Dunkirker; he "in peril of strangers," they not of strangers only but of their own household, their servants and factors; he "in peril of the sea," they both of the tempest at the sea, and the Publican on land; he "in peril of the wilderness," that is, of wild beasts, they not only of the wild beast called the sychophant, but of the tame beast too called the flatterer; he in danger "of false brethren," and so are they in peril of certain false brethren called wilful bankrupts, and of certain other called deceitful lawyers.[1]

Much of the style is highly colloquial. The sermon is filled with such expressions as "cobweb laws," "cobweb divinity," "cup-shotten wisdom," and "Westminster Hall moths," and it is enriched by homely proverbs: "As riseth our good, so riseth our blood"; "many sons roast not that their fathers got in hunting." Even Andrewes's use of Scripture has a colloquial flavor, as in this reference to the Pharisees: 'which after they have heard the charge do, as they did at Christ . . . jest and scoff, and make themselves merry with it, and wash it down with a cup of sack." His use of classical material is also colloquial, as in his description of the tree that Pliny speaks of, "the leaves of it as broad as any target, but the fruit no bigger than a bean—to talk targets and to do beans."

Above all, the congregation must have been conscious of a vividly dramatic voice. The tone of the preacher frequently shifts, adapting itself to the different requirements of the message. At times, Andrewes addresses his congregation in a directly personal way, as in his informal comment on the progress of the sermon: "I shall never get out of this point if I break not from it." And he gives voice to thoughts which may lurk in the minds of some members of the congregation, a practice which he would frequently return to in his later sermons. Here he takes the voice of the highminded man, scorning the preacher: "Tush, he doth prate, these things shall not come upon me, though I walk still according to the stubborness of mine own heart." His voice is highly emotional as he charges the congregation to fulfill their various duties; throughout the sermon, he is much bolder in addressing his special audience than he would be later in preaching to his court congregation.

In its themes, the sermon looks back to the Middle Ages and the earlier sixteenth century. Andrewes's elaborate attack on pride early in the sermon, and his recurring references to the transitoriness of the things of this world, especially riches, later on, are thoroughly medieval in spirit, as is his brief attack on usury, which he calls "the devil's alchemistry." In comparing the proud man with the poor man, Andrewes develops the traditional theme of Death as the great leveler in a passage which is similar in spirit to Donne: "and within a few years when you die, if a man come with a joiner and measure all that you carry with you, they shall carry away with them as much; and within a few years after, a man shall not be able to discern between the shoulder-blade of one of them and one of you."[2]

The elaborate, spirited attack on the papacy near the end of the sermon is consistent with the controversial spirit of the earlier sixteenth century: "seeing the Pope doth as he doth: that is, as he hath dispensed with the oath and duty of subjects of their Prince against the fifth commandment; with the murder, both violent and with dags [daggers], and secret with poison, of the sacred persons of Princes, against the sixth; with the uncleanness of the stews, and with incestuous marriages, against the seventh; so now of late, with the abomination of simony against the eighth . . . seeing thus do the Papists . . . to redeem the orderly disposing them to the Church's good, were a special way for you rich men to do good in these days."[3]

Like all of Andrewes's later sermons, the "Spittal Sermon" is effectively organized. Each section of the long text is thoroughly developed and carefully applied to the congregation, and the sermon reaches a climax in the last paragraph before the benediction with its vivid glimpse of the judgment day and its emotional application of the subject to the congregation: "Beloved, when your life shall have an end, as an end it shall have, when the terror of death shall be upon you; when your soul shall be cited to appear before God, *in novissimo*; I know and am perfectly assured all these things will come to mind again, you will perceive and feel that which possibly now you do not . . . provide for that day, and provide for eternal life. It will not come yet it is true, it will be long in coming; but when it comes, it will never have an end."[4]

Andrewes's "Spittal Sermon" provides a good introduction to his later sermons. The use of antitheses, the colloquial style, the dramatic speaking voice, the thorough development of each section of the text, and the careful organization of the whole work are characteristics which Andrewes would practice all through his preaching career.

II *The Miscellaneous Sermons*

In the collected edition of Andrewes's sermons, eleven of them, including the "Spittal Sermon," appear under the title "Certain Sermons Preached at Sundry Times, Upon Several Occasions," and this title aptly indicates the miscellaneous character of the grouping. All the sermons, except the one preached before Parliament in 1621, represent Andrewes's early work. Six were preached during the reign of Queen Elizabeth and five during King James's reign. Whereas the "Spittal Sermon" elaborately develops the scriptural text, the other sermons in the group are essentially expositions of topics. Six of them focus on religious subjects and four are primarily political. These sermons are more interesting as revelations of Andrewes's completely traditional religious and political beliefs than they are as examples of his preaching style.

The subjects of the religious sermons are varied: absolution (1600), justification (1600), God's use of the plague as punishment (1603), and putting the word of God into practice (1607). Of special interest are the two sermons in the group, preached in 1592, from Andrewes's early ministry, when he was vicar of the Parish Church of Saint Giles, Cripplegate. The sermon entitled "Of the Worshipping of Imaginations," preached on January 9, is a defense of the Church against what Andrewes considers false beliefs or "imaginations." In the course of the sermon, he touches on beliefs affecting all three parts of the service of the Church: the sermon, the Eucharist, and prayer. He defends the Church's practice of using Latin and Greek words, the Apocrypha, the Talmud, and heathen writings in sermons. He regards the Eucharist as both Sacrament and sacrifice, describing the Sacrament as "the partaking of Christ's true body." And in discussing prayer he holds the middle course, objecting both to the Catholic practice of praying in a language which the people do not understand and to those at the other extreme (the Puritans) who pray long extemporaneous prayers that reject any set liturgy. He also dismisses the Puritan system of government: "But not long since, some have fancied another, [form of fellowship] that should consist of Lay-elders, Pastors, and Doctors, and whether of Deacons too is not fully agreed yet. Which device is pressed now upon our Church, not as a form of more convenience than that it hath, but as one absolutely necessary, and of our Saviour Christ's own only institution, which maketh it the less sufferable."[5]

In the sermon entitled "Of the Lawfulness and Form of Swearing," delivered on June 11, 1592, Andrewes again keeps the middle course, defending the use of the oath against the Anabaptist's objection to all forms of swearing, and attacking the opposite, licentious spirit of the man who swears excessively. His attack on swearing is medieval in spirit, as he describes men who "in tabling-houses, at their game, blaspheme the name of God most grievously; not content to swear by Him whole, dismember Him and pluck Him in pieces, that they may have oaths enough."[6]

Of the four political sermons in the group, two focus on the subject of monarchy. In his sermon delivered at the Elizabethan court at Whitehall on November 15, 1601, on the text "Give therefore to Caesar the things which are Caesar's" (Matthew 22:21), Andrewes develops the theme of the monarch as God's "secondary means in the government of mankind." He declares that God has associated Caesar with Himself "in the high and heavenly work of the preservation of all our lives, persons, estates, and goods, in safety, peace, and quietness." The doctrine of Christian obedience to secular authority is stated in its extreme form: " 'the powers that are are ordained of God,' though Tiberius or Nero have the powers. It is not the man, it is 'the ordinance of God' we owe and perform our subjection to. We yield it not to Tiberius, but to Caesar." Andrewes concludes with an eloquent tribute to Queen Elizabeth, "above any Caesar of them all; who hath exalted Him Whom Tiberius crucified, and professed Him with hazard of her estate and life, Whom they persecuted in all bloody manner."[7]

Over four years later, Andrewes again developed the theme of monarchy in a sermon preached before King James on March 24, 1606, the third anniversary of his accession. The text is "In those days, there was no king in Israel, but every man did that which was good in his own eyes" (Judges 17:6), and the sermon progresses from a description of the misfortunes which befall a nation where there is no king to a discussion of the benefits a king bestows, the chief one being his championing of true religion. Near the end of the sermon, Andrewes develops the familiar theme of Christian obedience to the Prince, even an evil one, as he declares "better any than an anarchy; better any one a King, than every one a King," and he then retells the fable of the lion: "Better one lion . . . than all the bears and wolves and wild beasts of the forest." The whole sermon is an extended compliment to King James on his accession day, and it concludes with references to Old Testament rulers, allowing the congregation to draw parallels from England's own history. Jeroboam, "no stranger in birth . . . but one addicted to strange religion," is perhaps Mary Tudor. Rehoboam, "well for his religion, but otherwise not able to advise himself, and so ready to be advised for the worse," is probably Edward VI.[8] The sermon ends with a tribute to King James as the British Solomon, and as Melchisedek, the king of peace.

III *Sermons Preached in Lent*

Six of Andrewes's sermons are in a group entitled "Sermons Preached in Lent"; five of them were preached before Queen Elizabeth in 1589, 1590, 1593, and 1594 and the sixth was delivered to the court at Greenwich in 1596. This group provides the largest representation of Andrewes's Elizabethan sermons. Although they were preached during Lent, none of them develops a subject particularly appropriate for the season. Four of the sermons provide especially interesting examples of Andrewes as an Elizabethan preacher.

The opening two sermons focus on the subject of monarchy rather than on the spiritual life. Like the sermons in the miscellaneous group, they provide a clear picture of Andrewes's completely traditional political beliefs. The sermon delivered on March 11, 1589, at Greenwich is one of Andrewes's earliest sermons before the queen; the text is "The earth and all the inhabitants thereof are dissolved: but I will establish the pillars of it" (Psalm 75:3). Andrewes affirms that the well-ordered commonwealth is upheld by the pillars of religion and justice, which are, in turn, upheld by the ruler; and throughout the sermon he uses the imagery of music as a metaphor for the well-ordered state. He is especially vivid in his description of the anarchy which results when there is no established government, "Without which . . . we should have no commonwealth, but a wild forest, where Nimrod and his crew would hunt and chase all others; no commonwealth, but a pond where the great fish would devour the small . . . no building, nor pillars, but a heap of stones."[9] This sermon, preached almost a year after the English victory over the Spanish Armada, has a patriotic undercurrent. Andrewes obviously meant the congregation to see a correspondence between Israel and England, and he perhaps intended them to draw a parallel between King David, who strengthened the kingdom made weak by King Saul, and Queen Elizabeth, who strengthened England after the reign of Mary Tudor.

The sermon preached before the queen at Greenwich on February 24, 1590, is based on the text "Thou didst lead Thy people like sheep, by the hand of Moses and Aaron" (Psalm 77:20). Again Andrewes focuses on the well-ordered commonwealth and the exaltedness of the monarch. The rod of government, like the rods of Moses and Aaron, is miraculous, since it is not natural for any man to endure the pains of ruling over others. Andrewes eloquently describes the burden of rule, and he makes a graceful application of the subject to the queen: "it is surely supernatural to endure that cark and care which the governors continually do—a matter that we inferiors can little skill of . . . Wherefore when we see that careful mind in a prince, I will use Moses' own words, to carry a people in her arms, as if she had conceived them in her womb, as no nurse, nor mother more tender . . . let us see God sensibly in it." The ruling of the people is as much a wonder as the calming of the sea. The most powerful passage in the sermon is Andrewes's denunciation of the uncontrolled multitude, the Bible furnishing him with examples of the people's folly, giddiness, brutishness, spite, malice, and head-strongness. Even the word "people" is evil: "And this is the people, *populus*. And surely, no evil can be said too much of this word people, if ye take it apart by itself, *populus* without *Tuus*, 'the people,' and not 'Thy people.' " Near the end of the sermon, Andrewes presents an exalted picture of the monarch, who unites the two distinct duties of Aaron and Moses, the Ecclesiastical and Civil, "as the two Cherubims did the ark, overspread and preserve every estate."[10] The popularity of this particular sermon with the Elizabethan courtiers was recalled eighteen years later by Sir John Harington: "he [Andrewes] made a sermon before the Queen long since, which was the most famous, of this text: 'Thou leddest Thy people like sheep by the hands of Moses and Aaron.' Which sermon, (though courtiers' ears are commonly so open, as it goes in at one ear, and out at the other,) yet it left an *aculeus* behind in many of all sorts. And Henry Noell, one of the greatest gallants of those times, sware as he was a gentleman, he never heard man speak with such a spirit."[11]

The sermon delivered before the queen at Saint James's Palace on March 30, 1593, focuses on the Gospel account of Judas' rebuke of Mary Magdalene for anointing Jesus' head. This sermon is interesting both for its theme and for its style. As in other sermons in the group, Andrewes presents an underlying correspondence between the biblical passage and contemporary England. He obviously intends a compliment to the queen in the parallels he draws between Mary's anointing Christ's body and those who bestow honor on Christ's mystical body, the Church. Near the end of the sermon, he rejoices in the prosperity, plenty, and peace of England; and he directly compliments the queen: "Verily, Christ hath anointed over us, and given us a most gracious sovereign, by whose happy and blessed reign we long have—and longer may He grant!—enjoyed both the inward and outward anointing."[12] The sermon is also of stylistic value, for it contains more examples of Andrewes's early euphuistic prose style than any other of his Elizabethan sermons. The following passage, paraphrasing Judas' condemnation of Mary's act, is set forth with elaborately balanced contrasts: "that that which is otherwise lavished upon one may be employed to the benefit of many; that these so many hundreds may be bestowed rather in nourishment, than in ointment; rather on necessary relief, than upon needless delight; rather on a continual good, than on a transitory smell; rather that many hungry bellies filled, than that one head anointed."[13] It is appropriate to recall that John Lyly, the most famous practitioner of euphuism, was an early admirer of Andrewes's preaching.

The sermon preached before the queen at Hampton Court on March 6, 1594, ranks with the Passion sermon of 1597 as Andrewes's greatest Elizabethan sermon. Twice in the sermon he calls preachers "the Lord's remembrancers," and the brief text "Remember Lot's Wife" (Luke 17:32) gives him the opportunity of constructing a memorial sermon on her unfortunate life. The key word is "remember," which keeps tolling throughout the sermon, the word with its Latin equivalents occurring sixty times. Lot's wife provides a warning for the congregation against the vice of faint virtue and an exhortation to the virtue of perseverance. The technique of constructing a whole sermon on an exemplum is rare for Andrewes, and he is effective both in presenting the story and in making the application to the congregation. The chief virtue of the sermon lies in the vivid, almost compassionate manner in which Andrewes recreates the character of Lot's wife, making her not only a type of human frailty, but also a human being. In recalling her fall into sin, he recreates the day: "The sun rose so clear and it was so goodly a morning, she repented she came away." He concisely describes her backsliding: "she began to tire and draw behind, and kept not pace with Lot and the Angels." He depicts her weariness and emphasizes the hardships of her past by cataloguing the places which she had formerly passed through: "She grew weary of trouble, and of shifting so oft. From Ur to Haran; thence to Canaan; thence, to Egypt; thence to Canaan again, then to Sodom, and now to Zoar; and that in her old days, when she would fainest have been at rest."[14] In a climactic passage, Andrewes concisely emphasizes the pathos of a woman who "fell after she had stood so long": "But this woman had continued now thirty years . . . This, this, is the grief, that she should persist all this time, and after all this time fall away. The rather, if we consider yet farther, that not only she continued many years, but sustained many things in her continuance, as being companion of Abraham and Lot in their exile, their travel, and all their affliction. This is the grief, that after all these storms in the broad sea well passed, she should in this pitiful manner be wrecked in the haven."[15]

Near the end of the sermon, Andrewes makes his most elaborate compliment to Queen Elizabeth, "who, like Zerubbabel, first by princely magnanimity laid the corner-stone in a troublesome time," contrasting her heroic perseverance with the faint virtue of Lot's wife. This fine sermon represents an impressive memorial to Lot's wife, to the queen, and to Andrewes himself as an Elizabethan preacher.

IV *Andrewes as Elizabethan Preacher*

In examining these early sermons of Lancelot Andrewes, delivered as the Elizabethan period was drawing to a close, it is helpful to determine to what extent they are characteristic of his age and in what ways they represent something new. This question can partially be answered by comparing Andrewes's sermons with those of the man who was probably the most popular preacher of the time: the "silver-tongued" Henry Smith.[16]

Smith was a moderate Puritan, his congregations were the citizens of London, and his last office was lecturer at the Church of Saint Clement Danes. Thirty-seven of his sermons were collected and published in 1592, a year after his death. Even the titles of Smith's sermons indicate the practical, didactic nature of his work: "The Young-man's Taske," "A Glasse for Drunkards," "The Art of Hearing," "A looking Glasse for Christians." Smith is part of the long tradition of English popular preaching, and one of his most characteristic devices is the homely example, used to convey his simple message as forcefully as possible to his congregation. The following comparison from "A Glasse for Drunkards" provides a characteristic example: "So no marvell though Noah had a longing to his owne grapes . . . following heerin the example of a curious cooke, which doth sip his broth to taste whether it bee well seasoned, that hee may amend it if he can, or amend the next: but as the flye by often dallying with the candle, at last scorcheth her wings with the flame: so taking, hee was taken, and at laste was drunke."[17] Andrewes never sounds like this. The differences between the two preachers may partially be explained by the diverse nature of their congregations, but there is also a more basic stylistic difference. Smith exemplifies an old tradition, but Andrewes represents something new.

Of all Andrewes's surviving sermons only the first, his Spittal Sermon preached in 1588, could be considered popular, but even here his congregation of the leading citizens of London was different from the lower classes composing Smith's congregations.[18] Although in this sermon Andrewes does use Smith's characteristic device of the homely example, he rarely employs this technique in his other surviving sermons. The methods of the two preachers are, in fact, markedly different. Where Smith uses the scriptural texts merely as starting points for his simple didactic lessons, Andrewes, even in his first surviving sermon, displays one of his most characteristic methods: the close analysis and expansive development of the scriptural text. And where Smith's sermons do not employ Latin and Greek quotations from the Church Fathers, Andrewes supports his appeals to the London citizens with frequent quotations from Augustine; his sermon, in fact, is filled with short Latin quotations from the Fathers and Scripture, and even contains a few Greek phrases. Although Andrewes's sermon is longer than most of Smith's, the reader never loses a sense of its organic structure; it possesses a definite beginning, elaborate development, and powerful conclusion. This careful sense of form is not evident in Smith's sermons, but it is the foundation of all Andrewes's work.

Andrewes's two surviving parish sermons, preached when he was vicar of Saint Giles, are even more strikingly different from those of Smith. Especially interesting is Andrewes's sermon "Of the Worshipping of Imaginations," preached in 1592, the same year in which Smith's sermons were first published. It is an excellent example not of the popular but of the learned sermon. It is essentially a lecture, a learned argument appealing to the congregation's reason. Andrewes's knowledge of the long tradition of the Christian church is evident, as he selects appropriate quotations from the Fathers to support his arguments. Once, he does not even translate the Latin, perhaps indicating his confidence in the learning of his congregation. If this sermon is characteristic of those parish sermons of Andrewes which have not survived, it certainly implies a highly intelligent congregation. Andrewes's appeal, here and elsewhere, is primarily to the intellect, whereas Smith's didactic sermons mainly appeal to the emotions. The concise description of "learned" Andrewes and "patheticall" Smith given by Gabriel Harvey, their contemporary, is certainly apt.[19]

Smith favors the simplest language and the plainest style, declaring in one of his sermons that "to preach simply is not to preach rudely, nor unlearnedly, nor confusedly, but to preach plainly and perspicuously, that the simplest man may understand what is taught, as if he did hear his name."[20] His paragraphs are often simple developments of homely metaphors, as in the following simile, illustrating the dependence of the congregation on the preacher: "As the little birdes pierce up their heades when their damme comes with meate, and prepare their beakes to take it, striving who shall catch most; now this lookes to be served, and now that lookes for a bit, and every mouth is open untill it be filled: so you are here like birdes, and we the damme, and the worde the foode, therefore you must present a mouth to take it."[21]

Although Andrewes's language is as simple as Smith's, his themes are more complex, his methods more varied, and his style strikingly different. Even in one of his earliest sermons, preached before the queen in 1589, he exhibits a fairly elaborate method of paragraph development. Beginning with the simple metaphor "God is a pillar," Andrewes intricately intertwines, balances, and develops the two themes of the pillars of the Commonwealth and the Trinity of God. In contrast to Smith's long Ciceronian sentences, Andrewes's paragraph, with its terse, short constructions, already exhibits the Senecan brevity which would later characterize his style: "God is a pillar; so is His most common name in the Hebrew—Adonai, 'My Pillar.' And His Son, a Rock; not only Peter's Rock, but David's Rock too; the Rock both of Church and Kingdom. And His Spirit, a Spirit not of holiness only and truth, but 'a Spirit of judgment' to them that sit on the throne; and 'a Spirit of strength for them that keep the battle from the gate.' "[22]

Smith's sermons are not witty; he favors neither wordplay nor farfetched imagery. Andrewes, however, uses wordplay even in his earliest surviving court sermon, preached before the queen on Ash Wednesday, 1589: "Out of which their destruction, Asaph frameth an instruction for us." "Therefore, that we set ourselves to seek before this *cum* come." And in his sermon on Mary's anointing, delivered before the queen in 1593, he defends Mary's act as "a dispensation" rather than "a dissipation"; and he puns on the word "perdition" three times, in describing Judas' condemnation of Mary: "the son of perdition talk of perdition." The first appearance of farfetched imagery occurs in his sermon on Lot's wife, preached in 1594, in which Andrewes briefly plays with the image of salt, but the real flourishing of this aspect of his style occurs later, in his sermons preached before King James.

While Henry Smith exemplifies the timeless tradition of popular preaching, Lancelot Andrewes represents a new style of English preaching which developed in the last decade of the sixteenth century, but which would flourish only briefly for a period of about fifty years. This style is learned rather than popular; it is characterized by a careful and elaborate development of the scriptural text, frequent Latin and Greek quotations and references to the Fathers, and a rigorous sense of structure. The paragraphs are composed of short, pithy sentences and phrases; and the style is witty both in its use of words and images. This singular preaching represents an intellectual and stylistic advance in English pulpit oratory. It is even possible that Andrewes may have originated this unique style, but it is certain that in utilizing it, he was a pioneer and its best exemplar.

CHAPTER 5

The Nativity Sermons

ANDREWES'S greatest sermons are those which celebrate the holy days of the Christian church: Christmas, Ash Wednesday, Good Friday, Easter, and Pentecost. Throughout all these sermons, he reveals a sensitivity to the special significance of each holy day, his reverence for the day equal to his reverence for the text. For him, the day represents a memorial of a sacred event which the texts recall and the sermons develop. Interestingly, the ideal of recurring days of commemoration is most beautifully expressed in one of Andrewes's secular sermons, his first Gunpowder sermon, delivered in 1606: "Of keeping in remembrance, many ways there be: among the rest this is one, of making days, set solemn days, to preserve memorable acts, that they be not eaten out by them, but even revived with the return of the year, and kept still fresh in continual memory."[1]

Of all Andrewes's sermons, the Nativity group is the most familiar to the modern reader, especially his sermon preached in 1622 on the Wise Men, which inspired T. S. Eliot's "The Journey of the Magi." On Christmas days between 1605 and 1624, Andrewes preached seventeen sermons before King James in the Royal Chapel at Whitehall. In the first collected edition of his sermons, published in 1629, this group is given prominence, appearing first.

I *The Central Event*

For Andrewes as for other Christians, the Incarnation is the central event in human history, and he declares in his early 1606 sermon: "All are as lines drawn from this centre, all in Him 'yea and Amen.' " Throughout these sermons, Andrewes gives his attention not only to this primary occasion but also to the lines proceeding from its center, both in time and in place: from the moment of

Christ's Nativity, Andrewes's imagination ranges backwards and forwards in time. In the course of the sermons, he looks back to Christ's first begetting "in the mind of His Father before all worlds," to the fall of Adam, and to the Old Testament foreshadowings and prophecies of the coming of the Messiah. He looks ahead to the ministry, suffering, death, Resurrection, and Ascension of Christ, and to His exaltation at the right hand of the Father. Each sermon in the group presents a journey in time, and many of them conclude with glimpses of eternity.

Andrewes's imagination also ranges throughout space. For example, in his sermon preached in 1614 on the text "Behold a Virgin shall conceive, and bear a Son," the section on the birth of Christ is considerably enhanced by his vivid description of the lines of influence extending throughout the universe: "So that this is . . . when He came forth 'as a Bridegroom out of His chamber, or as the Sun from His tabernacle to run His race.' And it was with a *visitavit ab alto*. Thence an angel cried *Ecce*, and sounded it on earth; and a star cried *Ecce*, and proclaimed it from Heaven. Poets in the West write of it; and wise men in the East saw it, and came a long journey upon it to see Him. And what did this *pariet* bring forth? No sooner born, but a multitude of heavenly soldiers sung 'Peace to the earth.' "[2]

The mystery of the Incarnation also stimulates Andrewes's imagination to range back and forth between the low and the high. The element of contrast is a pervasive technique in his sermons, giving them much of their richness. In contrasting the humble sign of the manger with the glorious message of the angel in his 1618 sermon on the shepherds, Andrewes declares, "It is a course this, the Holy Ghost began it here at His birth . . . 'to couple low and high together, and to temper things mean and usual with others as strange every way.' "[3] As early as the first Nativity sermon preached in 1605, Andrewes couples "low and high together" in a striking paragraph which contrasts the abodes of Angels and men: "They, Heavenly Spirits, Angels of Heaven; that is, their place of abode is in Heaven above. Ours is here below in the dust, *inter pulices et culices, tineas, arcaneas, et vermes;* Our place is here 'among fleas and flies, moths and spiders, and crawling worms.' There is our place of dwelling."[4] And the remaining sermons in the group are filled with contrasts between the high and low, the great and the little, the divine and the human, Heaven and Earth, the Divine Son and the Human Child, the Word and the flesh, the message of the angel and the sign of the manger, birth and death. Indeed, death is just as prominent as birth in the Nativity sermons, for they also contain some of Andrewes's most powerful passages on Christ's Passion.

II *Content and Style*

Andrewes proclaims the contrast between the great and the small again in his sermon preached in 1615 on "little Bethlehem": "how huge an oak from how small an acorn," where he declares that "God seems to take delight . . . to bring *maxima de minimis;* great out of little." It is an interesting example of the close relationship between Andrewes's theme and his style that many passages in the Nativity sermons could themselves be described as deriving great things from small, "maxima de minimis." His paragraphs often compress much matter into little space, a characteristic which T. S. Eliot probably was referring to when he wrote of Andrewes's "relevant intensity."[5] Indeed, several of Andrewes's most vivid passages are those in which the whole life of Christ is compressed within the small compass of a single paragraph, as in the following passage from his sermon preached in 1611 on the text "And the word was made flesh":

> The flesh of an infant. What, *Verbum infans*, the Word an infant? The Word, and not be able to speak a word? How evil agreeth this! This He put up. How born, how entertained? In a stately palace, cradle of ivory, robes of estate? No; but a stable for His palace, a manger for His cradle, poor clouts for His array. This was His beginning. Follow Him farther, if any better afterward; what flesh afterward? *Sudans et algens*, in cold and heat, hungry and thirsty, faint and weary. Is His end any better? that maketh up all: what flesh then? *Cujus livore sanati*, black and blue, bloody and swollen, rent and torn, the thorns and nails sticking in His flesh; and such flesh He was made.[6]

In no other group of Andrewes's sermons is his enthusiasm for antithetical constructions so appropriate to his message as in the sermons on the Incarnation, which present the great paradox of God's becoming man. This paradox is developed by the antitheses in the following brief paragraph, in which the two natures of Christ are contrasted in the Human Child and the Divine Son: "All along His life you shall see these two. At His birth; a cratch [manger] for the Child, a star for the Son; a company of shepherds viewing the Child, a choir of Angels celebrating the Son. In His life; hungry

Himself, to shew the nature of the Child; yet 'feeding five thousand,' to shew the power of the Son. At His death; dying on the cross, as the 'Son of Adam;' at the same time disposing of Paradise, as the 'Son of God.' "[7]

The appearance of an Infinite God in a finite world is the central paradox of the Incarnation which permeates all the sermons in the group. Andrewes most fully explores this paradox in his sermon preached in 1609 on the text "When the fulness of time was come, God sent His Son": "To make Him any thing is to mar Him, be it what it will be. To send Him made, is to send Him marred, and no better. . . . If God make Him anything, He must be a thing made, a creature, and that is a great disparagement. So that howsoever the time is the fuller for this, He is the emptier; . . . 'the fulness of time is his emptiness;' the exalting of that, His abasing."[8]

In the course of the sermons, this "great disparagement" is presented most forcefully, not only through Andrewes's antithetical style but also through his vigorous imagery. The most vivid and extended imagery on Christ's abasement occurs in the sermon preached in 1612, in which, at the climactic discussion of Christ's purging of man's sins, Andrewes powerfully blends the image of the Divine Prince with that of the Divine Physician: "as if a great prince should go into an hospital, to visit and look on a loathsome diseased creature . . . 'to make the medicine, and be the medicine.' " Later, in depicting the Passion, the imagery becomes more extravagant: "The Physician slain, and of His Flesh and Blood a receipt made, that the patient might recover!" Near the end of the sermon, Andrewes emphasizes the degradation with a familiar image and a pun: "when He That was 'the brightness of His Father's glory' should be so eclipsed. He that sits on the throne thus be thrown in a manger."[9]

III *Andrewes and the Word*

Andrewes's favorite image for presenting the paradox of Christ's abasement is "the *Verbum infans,* the Word without a word; the eternal Word not able to speak a word," a figure he borrowed from Bernard and which he develops four times in the course of his sermons. The paradox of the Word's becoming flesh provided Andrewes with his greatest opportunity to display his own affection for the word. In his sermon preached in 1611 on the text "and the Word was made flesh," Andrewes pays high tribute to the human word by comparing its procreation to the pure conception of the Divine

Word: "For there is not in all the world a more pure, simple, inconcrete procreation than that whereby the mind conceiveth the word within it, by *dixit in corde*. For in itself and of itself doth the mind produce it without help of any mixture of ought, without any passion stirring or agitation at all. Such was the issue of the Word eternal."[10] Andrewes's enthusiasm for words reveals itself in many ways. In creating sermons on the Nativity texts, he frequently uses single words to color whole passages, even entire sermons. Much of the sermon preached in 1606 develops the paired words "child" and "son"; the entire sermon preached in 1609 is constructed on the single word "fulness";[11] and the sermon delivered the following year focuses on the word "joy." In the first Nativity sermon, preached in 1605 on the text "sed semen Abrahae apprehendit," the most vigorous section is a development of the word "apprehendit" which Andrewes expands dramatically to depict Christ's earnest pursuit of man, a brief version of the theme of the Hound of Heaven. In the famous Wise Men sermon preached in 1622, the reader may overlook how much the single word "star," from the text, colors the whole sermon, the word and its equivalents appearing fifty times.

On occasion, Andrewes plays with words, as in his famous word dissection in the sermon preached in 1614 on Isaiah 7:14: "Behold, a virgin shall conceive, and bear a Son, and she shall call His name Immanuel." Here, he breaks up the word "Immanuel" into its three parts. "El," "anu," and "im," endows them with life, and presents them in a brief narrative:

> and so then have we three pieces. 1. *El*, the mighty God; 2. and *anu*, we, poor we—poor indeed if we have all the world beside if we have not Him to be with us; 3. and *Im*, which is *cum*,and the *cum* in the midst between *nobis* and *Deus*, God and us—to couple God and us; thereby to convey the things of the one to the other. . . .
>
> So upon the point, in these three pieces there be three persons so a second kind of Trinity—God, We, and Christ. *El* is God, *anu* we; for Christ nothing left but *Im*, that is *Cum*, or "with." For it is He that maketh the unity in this Trinity; maketh God with us, and us with God; and both, in and by Him, to our eternal comfort and joy.[12]

Not only does Andrewes give birth to this "second kind of Trinity" but he also coins new words from the old: "if it be not *Immanu-el*, it will be *Immanu-hell;* and that no other place will fall, I fear me, to our share. Without Him this we are. What with Him? Why, if we have Him, and God by Him, we need no more; *Immanu-el* and *Immanu-all*."

Two years later Andrewes again endowed words with life in the sermon he preached in 1616 on a text from Psalm 85. Here, perhaps following the Venerable Bede, he makes Mercy, Truth, Righteousness, and Peace female and presents them as characters in a little drama. In one scene, Righteousness and Mercy engage in a spirited dialogue on the conflicting claims of Justice and Mercy: "What shall become of me, said Righteousness? What use of justice if God will do no justice, if He spare sinners? And what use of me, saith Mercy; if He spare them not? Hard hold there was, inasmuch as *perii nisi homo moriatur,* said Righteousness, 'I die, if he die not.' And *perii, nisi misericordiam consequatur,* said Mercy, 'if he die I die too.' " Then all four characters separate, Righteousness fleeing to Heaven. Before the coming of Christ, "Righteousness had no prospect, no window open this way. She turned away her face, shut her eyes, clapped to the casement, would not abide so much as to look hither—at us, a sort of forlorn sinners;—not vouchsafe us once the cast of her eye."[13] But at the birth of Christ, she looks down from Heaven, beats out a window, and comes down to earth, joining Peace, Mercy, and Truth at the Child-house where she kisses Peace. This sermon provides the most prolonged use of personification in any of Andrewes's sermons, presenting a dramatic allegory unique in his work.

IV *Sermons on the Shepherds and Wise Men*

Andrewes did not preach the Christmas sermon in 1617 because he was sick from "a sodain surfet of porke, that had almost caried him away."[14] The next year, however, he preached the first of the four Christmas sermons which bring the Nativity group to a grand climax. These are the two pairs of sermons on the shepherds and the Wise Men preached on Christmas in 1618, 1619, 1620, and 1622. Andrewes's imagination was so stimulated by the two texts that in each case he could not confine himself to a single sermon but extended the development of the text to two.

The four sermons are a culmination of the whole Nativity group, developing many of the themes which had gone before. For example, the sermon preached in 1618 on Luke 2:12, "And this shall be a sign unto you; ye shall find the child swaddled, and laid in a cratch," is a development of the dominant theme of the coupling of the low and the high which Andrewes proclaims in the introduction to the sermon. Andrewes gives little attention to the shepherds, emphasizing instead the contrast between the shame of the sign of the manger and the glory of the song of the angels. The entire sermon is constructed on striking contrasts which contribute to its strength. Birth and death are powerfully juxtaposed in a passage uniting the manger and the cross: "We may well begin with Christ in the cratch; we must end with Christ on the Cross. The cratch is a sign of the Cross. They that write *de re rustica,* describe the form of making a cratch cross-wise. The scandal of the cratch is a good preparative to the scandal of the Cross. To be swaddled thus as a child, doth that offend? What then, when ye shall see Him pinioned and bound as a malefactor? To lie in a manger, is that so much? How then, when ye shall see Him hang on the cross?"[15]

The contrast between low and high is emphasized by wordplay: "He that cometh here in clouts, He will come in the clouds one day." And in depicting the "great disparagement," forceful imagery contributes to the power of the sermon as in this extended conceit on the sun in eclipse: "The sun eclipsed, the sun in sackcloth; that is *signum in sole,* 'the sign indeed.' And that is the sign here: 'the Sun of Righteousness' entering into His eclipse begins to be darkened in his first point, the point of His Nativity."[16] It is in this sermon too that the paradox of the *Verbum Infans* receives its final and most eloquent development: "*Verbum infans,* the Word without a word; the eternal Word not able to speak a word . . . 'He,' that . . . 'taketh the vast body of the main sea, turns it to and fro, as a little child, and rolls it about with the swaddling bands of darkness;'—He to come thus into clouts, Himself! . . . There lieth He, the Lord of glory without all glory. Instead of a palace, a poor stable; of a cradle of state, a beast's cratch; no pillow but a lock of hay; no hangings but dust and cobwebs; no attendants, but *in medio animalium.*"[17]

In shifting from the sign of the manger to the song of the angels even the description of the Heavenly Choir is enhanced by contrast: "A sign this and a strange one, this conjunction, *species praeliantium,* and *voces cantantium,* 'the habit of war,' and 'the song of peace.' Soldiers make a camp, come to fight; these make a choir, come to sing. They are not in the habit of choir-men yet they sing; they are in the habit of men of war, yet sing of peace."[18]

The conclusion naturally applies the contrast underlying the whole sermon to a description of the Eucharist which the congregation will soon receive: "For Christ in the Sacrament is not altogether unlike Christ in the cratch. To the cratch we may well liken the husk or outward symbols of it. Outwardly it seems little worth but it is rich of contents, as was the crib this day with Christ in it. For what are they, but *infirma et egena elementa*, 'weak and poor elements' of themselves? yet in them find we Christ. Even as they did this day *in praesepi jumentorum panem Angelorum*, 'in the beasts crib the food of Angels:' which very food our signs both represent, and present unto us."[19]

The sermon preached the next year, 1619, on the same text shifts from the manger and choir to the song of the angels. For the modern reader it is less interesting than its predecessor, appearing somewhat belabored in the development of the text, especially in the overly long discussion of the words "glory" and "peace," but it does provide a good example of a work effectively unified by the dominant music imagery which permeates the sermon from beginning to end. In dividing into three parts the text "Glory be to God in the high Heavens, and peace upon earth, and towards men good-will," Andrewes's language is technical: "But if, as it is most proper, we consider the parts as in a song, the three will well agree with the scale in music. 1. *In excelsis*, on high, *hypate;* 2. on earth, *nete;* 3. and men, howsoever they come in last, they make *mese*, 'the mean.' " Glory, Peace and Good Will are "the three notes of the song in this anthem."[20] Musical imagery recurs throughout the sermon, and near the end Andrewes makes the application to the congregation in musical terms: "And now ye have heard all the parts, what shall we do with this song? Sing it. . . . Time in music is much. And if we will keep time with the Angels, do it when they do it—this day they did it; and what fitter time to sing it than the day it was first sung."[21] The final paragraph glimpses the future eternal harmony between men and angels.

The two sermons on the Wise Men crown the whole Nativity group. Although one Christmas intervened between their delivery, they are, in fact, an artistic whole, the 1620 sermon providing a splendid introduction to the later, more familiar work. The opening sentence furnishes a concise transition from the sermons on the shepherds to the new subject: "We pass now this year from the shepherds and the Angels, to the wise men and their star," and Andrewes quickly reveals his enthusiasm: "We pass . . . but from the less to the greater; for of the twain this is the greater. Greater in itself, greater to us." After an unusually elaborate introduction and an intricate division, the sermon focuses on the persons of the text, the Wise Men, but instead of physically describing them Andrewes presents them as types: Gentiles, Eastern sinners, great persons, and wise men. In discussing their greatness, he makes a graceful compliment to the king in his congregation—"To Kings, to sceptres, Christ cannot but be well inclined"—and in presenting their wisdom he makes an eloquent defense of heathen knowledge: "there is no truth at all in human learning or philosophy that thwarteth any truth in Divinity, but sorteth well with it and serveth it, and all to honour Him Who saith of Himself *Ego sum Veritas*, 'I am the Truth' "[22]

The whole subject is so rich that Andrewes declares at the beginning of the application that he will be able to proceed in the development of the text no further than the word "Venerunt." Perhaps he intended to save the subject of the journey for fuller development in a later sermon, but he does focus his conclusion on the word "Venerunt,' which, with its equivalents, rings out forty-seven times; and he constructs a whole paragraph on the journey, certain passages anticipating the famous description in the later sermon: "They came a long journey, no less than twelve days together. They came an uneasy journey, for their way lay through Arabia Petraea, and the craggy rocks of it. And they came a dangerous journey through Arabia Deserta too, and the black 'tents of Kedar' there, then famous for their robberies, and even to this day. And they came now, at the worst season of the year."[23]

The sermon concludes with an application of the subject of the journey to the congregation's coming participation in the Sacrament of the Eucharist, and Andrewes recalls an old tradition: "in the old Ritual of the Church we find that on the cover of the canister, wherein was the Sacrament of His body, there was a star engraven, to shew us that now the star leads us thither, to His body there."[24] The last paragraph continues the application, the word "come" ringing out three times, and the vision of the journey expands to brief glimpses of the Heavenly Kingdom. This sermon, with its elaborate development to its grand conclusion, is one of Andrewes's finest.

The sermon on the Wise Men preached two years later, in 1622, is Andrewes's most famous work. This sermon contains so many echoes of its predecessor that it almost appears as if Andrewes had the earlier sermon before him. Like it, the 1622 sermon is elaborately constructed, the division alone extending to two pages in the printed text. After considering several possible divisions, Andrewes proclaims that "The text is of a star, and we may make all run on a star"; he declares that there are three stars in the text; and he unexpectedly develops the sermon not on the heavenly star but on the star of faith in the hearts of the Wise Men. The whole sermon is constructed on an elaborate five-point division, comparing the five beams of the Wise Men's faith: their saying, seeing, coming, asking, and worshiping, to the five points of the star.

Appropriately, the famous passage in the *Venimus* section describing their journey occurs in the center of the sermon. Although the description is brief, it is filled with flashes of detail: "This was nothing pleasant, for through deserts, all the way waste and desolate . . . for over the rocks and crags of both Arabias, specially Petraea, their journey lay . . . lying through the midst of the 'black tents of Kedar,' a nation of thieves and cut-throats; to pass over the hills of robbers, infamous then, and infamous to this day. . . . It was no summer progress. A cold coming they had of it at this time of the year, just the worst time of the year to take a journey, and specially a long journey in. The ways deep, the weather sharp, the days short, the sun farthest off, *in solstitio brumali*, 'the very dead of winter.' "[25]

From this central event, Andrewes's imagination expands, as it so often does throughout the sermons of the Nativity group. He touches other biblical journeys of Abraham, the Queen of the South, and the Ethiopian eunuch, and he briefly passes from the East to the West in his references to Pliny's and Vergil's comments on the prophetic star. In discussing the worship of the Wise Men at Christ's birth his imagination takes him to the mock worship at Christ's death in a passage which compares Christ's persecution to a Christmas game: "And at His death, the other Herod, he sought Him too; but it was that he and his soldiers might make themselves sport with Him. Such seeking there is otherwhile. And such worshipping; as they in the judgment-hall worshipped Him with *Ave Rex*, and then gave Him a bob blindfold."[26]

Versatility of language also contributes to the sermon's vitality, from the colloquial level of the proverb and common saying ("The nearer the Church, the farther from God"; "We put Him to His thirds"), through wordplay ("his worshipping will prove worrying"; "more like to be abhorred than adored"), to the exalted level of much of the description. In none of Andrewes's sermons does the voice of the preacher shift more dramatically. It is playfully earnest as it speaks the imagined objections of slothful members of the congregation: "We love to make no very great haste. . . . Why should we? Christ is no wild-cat. What talk ye of twelve days? And if it be forty days hence, ye shall be sure to find His Mother and Him; she cannot be churched till then. What needs such haste? . . . Best get us a new Christmas in September; we are not like to come to Christ at this feast. Enough for *venimus*."[27] It is ironic as it reveals contemporary pride: "For they in the East were nothing so wise, or well seen, as we in the West are now grown. We need call no Scribes together, and get them tell us, 'where.' Every artisan hath a whole Synod of Scribes in his brain, and can tell where Christ is better than any learned man of them all."[28] And the voice of the preacher reaches its most exalted level when it becomes the voice of Christ, dramatically concluding the sermon. This speech provides the most magnificent end to any of Andrewes's sermons, and it is more daring than is commonly realized since it depicts Christ in the last days not as an object of worship, but as a worshiper: "for I have seen their star shining and shewing forth itself by the like beams; and as they came to worship Me, so am I come to do them worship. A *venite* then, for a *venimus* now. Their star I have seen, and give them a place above among the stars. They fell down: I will lift them up, and exalt them. And as they offered to Me, so am I come to bestow on them, and to reward them with the endless joy and bliss of My Heavenly Kingdom."[29] It is, indeed, appropriate that Eliot singled out this one sermon of Andrewes for immortality, since in its impressive structure, its range of vision, and its richness of language it is characteristic of the whole Nativity group and representative of Andrewes's best work.

After the second of the Wise Men sermons, the sermon preached the next year (1623) provides an appropriate summary of the whole Nativity group. The text itself is a recapitulation: "That in the dispensation of the fulness of the times, He might gather together into one all things, both which are in Heaven, and which are in earth, even in Christ" (Ephesians 1:10), and the sermon rehearses just those themes which had been previously developed in the group. Here the paradox of the Incarnation receives its final statement: "*Verbum in principio* 'the eternal,' mighty, great 'Word' became *Verbum abbreviatum*. . . . He that 'the Heavens are but His span,' abbreviate into a child of a span long."[30] And in developing for the last time the basic theme of the conjunction of Heaven and Earth at Christ's Nativity, Andrewes concisely summarizes the subjects of his last four sermons: "look there comes a choir of Angels down, there comes a new star forth to represent the things in Heaven, there comes together a sort of shepherds and there is gathering to them a troop of great princes from the East to represent the things on earth, which consist, as these do, of high and low, noble and base, wise and simple; all to celebrate and make shew of this gathering."[31] The concluding paragraph of the sermon expands into a glimpse of the fullness of eternity, and the last sentence makes a concise application of the subject of the Christmas season to the congregation: "that as the year, so the fulness of our lives may end in a Christmas, a merry joyful feast, as that is!"

The final Nativity sermon, preached in 1624, is of special interest because it is also the final surviving sermon which Andrewes delivered. Andrewes describes the text itself as a sermon: "I will preach the law, whereof the Lord said to Me: Thou art My Son, this day have I begotten Thee" (Psalm 2:7). Appropriately, this last sermon is in the nature of a valediction, and Andrewes's voice is filled with earnestness and urgency as he emphasizes, perhaps for the last time, the profound responsibility both of the preacher and the congregation.

Altogether, the Nativity group of sermons is remarkable for its breadth and variety. The paradox of Christ's Incarnation and Nativity, with all of its abundant associations, was especially congenial to Andrewes's distinctive style, and the Nativity sermons remain the most enduring monument of his pulpit oratory.

CHAPTER 6

Sermons of Repentance and Fasting and Sermons of the Passion

I *Sermons of Repentance and Fasting*

ANDREWES'S eight sermons entitled "Sermons of Repentance and Fasting" extend over a wider range of years than any other group. The first three sermons were preached before Queen Elizabeth on Ash Wednesdays in 1589,[1] 1599, and 1602; the next four before King James at Whitehall on Ash Wednesdays between 1619 and 1623; and the last sermon, prepared to be preached but never delivered, is dated 1624. This group is not as homogeneous as the sermons preached on the great Christian festivals; the sermons are commemorations of a season rather than celebrations of a day, and they focus not on the life of Christ but on the spiritual life of the Christian. Instead of being expositions of texts, therefore, they are exhortations to the congregation for repentance and the amendment of life, and their themes are those of seeking the Lord (Sermon One), keeping from wickedness (Sermon Two), turning to God (Sermons Three and Four), fasting (Sermons Four and Five), shunning hypocrisy (Sermon Six), and bringing forth fruits (Sermons Seven and Eight). Andrewes concisely states the purpose of these sermons in the one preached in 1623, the last of the group to be delivered: "The only true praise of a sermon is, some evil left, or some good done upon the hearing of it."[2]

Of the three Elizabethan sermons the second, preached at Richmond in 1599, is the most interesting. It is one of Andrewes's few occasional sermons, given for the forthcoming expedition of the Earl of Essex against the Irish rebels. Near the beginning of the sermon Andrewes prays that the host "may happily go, and thrice happily come again, with joy and triumph to her sacred Majesty, honour to themselves, and general contentment to the whole land,"[3] a hope which was not fulfilled. Near the sermon's end he makes a complimentary association between Queen Elizabeth and Deborah, the heroic judge of Israel. The text is appropriate for the occasion: "When thou goest out with the host against thine enemies, keep thee then from all wickedness" (Deuteronomy 23:9), and the sermon is traditional in its justification of war as being both lawful and holy, the most just when directed against rebellious subjects. War is God's fearful rod, "an act . . . of justice corrective, whose office is to punish sin."[4] Throughout the sermon, Andrewes ingeniously balances war (justice inflicted on others) with repentance (self-inflicted correction).

The four sermons preached before King James are elaborate exhortations to the congregation. Both the 1619 and 1621 sermons discuss fasting, and the latter sermon, on the text "When you fast, look not sour as the hypocrites," is essentially a lecture on a practice which must have encountered opposition since Andrewes declares that he chose the text "to stop the mouths of them that malign it." He defends fasting with numerous citations from the Church Fathers, especially Augustine and Tertullian; and he strongly supports the virtue of fasting for the Christian's spiritual life, probably basing his comments on his own spiritual experiences. This sermon, in fact, provides an interesting glimpse of the quality of spiritual life which Andrewes himself must have lived, and which is most clearly revealed in his *Devotions*. He declares that, for the Christian, fasting provides a "with-drawing place" and that it is "a special friend to prayer, to feather it, to put a vigour or fervour into it . . . We feel . . . that dull is our devotion and our prayers full of yawning, when the brain is thick with the vapour and the heart pressed down with the charge of the stomach."[5]

In the following year, 1622, Andrewes preached on the last portion of the text, "look not sour as the hypocrites," and the sermon is a vigorous attack on hypocrisy. The sermon's dominant metaphor of the world as a stage belongs to a long tradition, extending from the classical period through Andrewes's own age. Andrewes makes an elaborate comparison between hypocrites and stage-players which extends to six pages in the printed text. He associates the "hypocrites" with the Latin word "histriones," "such as in disguised attire and hair present themselves on a stage, and there oft represent those whom, God knows, they are far from." And he fully develops the familiar metaphor: "the heathen man long since observed, that *Mundus scena*, that in his conceit 'the world for all the world was like a stage or theatre,' scarce a true face in it, all in a manner personate." Andrewes mentions biblical "histriones," such as Judas, the Pharisees, and that "*Roscius in scena,* 'the master hyprocrite of all,' " Satan. He humorously applies the comparison to the congregation, referring to "sermon hypocrites" as those whose bodies are in church while their hearts are elsewhere and who " 'hear a song of one that hath a pleasing voice,' and no more comes of the sermon than of the song." The godliness of hypocrites, who merely play religion, is "scenical, theatrical, histrionical," and their end is "to be magnified up and down the people's mouth, that is even the *consummatum est* of all this stage-devotion."[6] This sermon, preached the same year as the great Wise Men sermon, is powerful in its singleminded attack on the sin of hypocrisy, infused throughout with the vitality of conviction.

The chief beauty of the Ash Wednesday sermons, however, is found in the scattered passages which describe the beauties of the natural world. The beginning of spring coincides with the beginning of Lent, and Andrewes frequently develops the parallel between Nature and Christian life. In his last surviving sermon preached to the queen in 1602, less than a year before her death, Andrewes's words are strangely prophetic: "now do these fowls return. Who knoweth whether he shall live to see them return any more? It may be the last spring, the last swallow-time, the last Wednesday of this name or nature we shall ever live to hear this point preached." And he emphasizes the importance of repentance by appealing to nature, which "itself seemeth to favour it, that at the rising of the year we should rise, and return when the zodiac returneth to the first sign."[7]

This same idea is also expanded in the sermon preached before King James in 1619 on the text "Turn you unto Me with all your heart" (Joel 2:12):

> for once a year all things turn. And that once is now at this time, for now at this time is the turning of the year. In Heaven, the sun in his equinoctial line, the zodiac and all the constellations in it, do now turn about to the first point. The earth and all her plants, after a dead winter, return to the first and best season of the year. The creatures, the fowls of the air, the swallow and the turtle, and the crane and the stork, "know their seasons," and make their just return at this time every year. Every thing now turning, that we also would make it our time to turn to God in.[8]

Imagery from nature is abundant in the last two sermons in the group, both of which are based on the same text: "Bring forth therefore fruit worthy amendment of life" (Matthew 3:7–8). In fact, the sermon preached in 1623 is constructed entirely on the image of fruit-bearing trees, and it reaches a powerful climax with the development of the "*ira ventura*" of the text in which the image of the fruit-bearing Christian is placed in the midst of the final day of wrath: "You need not fly, you need not stir no more than a tree, but keep your standing, and bear your fruit, and it shall not come near you but over you as did the destroying Angel their houses in Egypt."[9] Finally, in his application to the congregation—after quoting from Vergil's *Eclogues* on the blossoming season, "*Nunc omnis parturit arbos*"—Andrewes sensitively describes the return of spring: "if we will keep time with the Heavens, now the Heavens return again to their first degree; it is turning time in Heaven. If with the fowls of Heaven, and them Christ bids us look to, they know their times just, and just at this time make their return, the poor swallows and all."[10] Andrewes's biographer Isaacson early notes his great love for Nature; and it is in the Sermons on Repentance and the Resurrection sermons, delivered each spring, that this enthusiasm is most clearly displayed.

II *Sermons of the Passion*

Only three of Andrewes's Passion sermons, preached on Good Friday, have been preserved. They are early works, preceding all the sermons in the Nativity, Resurrection, and Pentecost groups. The first sermon was preached at the Elizabethan court in 1597 while the other two were delivered before King James at Whitehall in 1604 and at Greenwich in 1605, when Andrewes was Dean of Westminster.

In no other group of sermons does Andrewes so distinctly recreate a scene; the Passion group is remarkable for its intensity of vision. In the first of these sermons, Andrewes succinctly presents the benefit of the day "which is dedicated to none other end, but even to lift up the Son of Man, as Moses did the serpent in the wilderness, that we may look upon Him and live."[11] Each of the texts for the three sermons provides an opportunity for the congregation to look closely at the Son of Man: "And they shall look upon Me, Whom they have pierced" (Zechariah 12:10); "Consider, and behold, if ever there were sorrow like My sorrow" (Lamentations 1:12); and "Looking unto Jesus the Author and Finisher of our faith . . . Who . . . endured the cross" (Hebrews 12:2). Throughout the sermons, the Passion is termed a spectacle, and the congregation is frequently urged to focus their attention as spectators on the scene. Andrewes declares in the final Passion sermon that "the Passion is a piece of perspective, and that we must set ourselves to see it if we will see it well, and not look superficially on it."[12] The Passion sermons are in the familiar tradition of the meditation or contemplation, and the spectacle of the crucifixion is recreated so that the preacher and the congregation will be spiritually uplifted.

In focusing on the spectacle, the sermons are most impressive in their language and in their use of concrete detail. In describing the piercing of Christ in the first sermon, Andrewes comments on the appropriateness of the word "transfixerunt," and in translating it he effectively repeats the word "through," perhaps intending to depict the increasing penetration of Christ's body:[13] "through and through; through skin and flesh, through hands and feet, through side and heart, and all; the deadliest and deepest wound, and of highest gradation."[14] In the same sermon he not only encourages the congregation to observe the scene, but he also makes them participants, even to the extent of crucifying Christ themselves; "So that it was the sin of our polluted hands that pierced His hands, the swiftness of our feet to do evil that nailed His feet, the wicked devices of our heads that gored His head, and wretched desires of our hearts that pierced His heart."[15] In a powerful passage in the second sermon, Andrewes forces the congregation to look on the spectacle of Christ's suffering body, calling their attention to every detail: "Our very eye will soon tell us no place was left in His body, where He might be smitten and was not. His skin and flesh rent with the whips and scourges, His hands and feet wounded with the nails, His head with the thorns, His very heart with the spear-point; all His senses, all His parts laden with whatsoever wit or malice could invent."[16] And the Passion as a spectacle, with the audience both watching and participating, is most vigorously depicted in the final sermon through the use of visual details and forceful verbs:

> Was it a tragedy, or a Passion trow? A Passion it was, yet by their behaviour it might seem a May-game. Their shouting and outcries, their harrying of Him about from Annas to Caiphas, from him to Pilate, from Pilate to Herod, and from him to Pilate again; one while in purple, Pilate's suit; another while in white, Herod's livery; nipping Him by the cheeks, and pulling off His hair; blindfolding Him and buffeting Him; bowing to Him in derision, and then spitting in His face;—was as if they had not the Lord of glory, but some idiot or dizard in hand.[17]

At the conclusion of this sermon, Andrewes reminds the congregation that they are not only spectators but also participants, running a race in the theater of this world with the saints and Christ Himself as spectators.

The imagery which Andrewes uses in depicting the spectacle of Christ on the cross is traditional. Christ is associated with Old Testament types: Isaac's offering, Joseph's selling, Israel's calling from Egypt, Josias' dying, and Zerubbabel's building of the temple. The most frequent image is Christ as Moses' brazen serpent, lifted up in the wilderness; and He is also compared to the Passover lamb, the leafless vine, the treader in the winepress, and the loadstone of love. Some of these images are developed in extensive passages. In both the first and third sermons, Andrewes employs the comparison of Christ's life with the "cervus matutinus" or "morning hart," an image based on a traditional inscription for Psalm 22, the Psalm of Passion. Interestingly, the passages in the two sermons are almost identical. In the first version, Christ is "a hart roused early in the morning, as from His very birth He was by Herod, hunted and chased all His life long, and this day brought to His end, and, as the poor deer, stricken and pierced through side, heart, and all."[18] Near the end of this sermon, Andrewes even applies this image to the Sacrament of the Eucharist: "There may we be partakers of the flesh of the Morning Hart, as upon this day killed."

The final Passion sermon is the longest, richest, and most elaborate in its development of the text. Here the imagery is more extravagant, too, as in Andrewes's description of Christ's Passion as a second baptism and in his depiction of Christ's stripes as lattices, His wounds as windows, and "the nails and spear-head . . . as keys to let us in," the last image taken from Bernard. Perhaps the most hyperbolic image is the comparison of Christ on the cross to the "Liber Charitatis" (The "Book of Love"), an image Andrewes had used in his first Passion Sermon but one he develops more fully here. Christ is "*Liber charitatis*. . . . Every stripe as a letter, every nail a capital letter. His *livores* as black letters, His bleeding wounds as so many rubrics, to shew upon record His love towards us."[19]

The Passion, like the Nativity, presents a paradox. The Nativity was an exaltation for man but an abasement for Christ, while the Passion, seemingly a degradation for Christ, was in reality an exaltation. Appropriately, near the end of the final Passion sermon, Andrewes passes in his development of the text from the degradation of the cross to the joy of exaltation, from Christ hanging on the cross to His sitting on the throne, from Christ as Author to Christ as Finisher. The Savior "went to His Passion with Psalms, and with such triumph and solemnity, as He never admitted all His life before." The key word is "joy," and Andrewes declares that joy is "the very life and soul of the Passion, and all besides but 'the anatomy' the carcass without it."[20] The conclusion provides a grand climax, not only to this sermon but to the whole Passion group.

Although only three of Andrewes's Passion sermons survive, the intensity of their vision places them with his best work. In his final Passion sermon, Andrewes declares that "Christ and His cross were never parted";[21] and in his Nativity and Resurrection sermons his imagination would frequently be stimulated by the spectacle of Christ on the cross, bringing to these sermons too some of their most striking passages.

CHAPTER 7

Sermons of the Resurrection

EIGHTEEN of Andrewes's Resurrection sermons survive, more than in any other group. Seventeen were preached before King James on Easter Sundays between 1606 and 1623, sixteen at Whitehall and one at Durham Cathedral in 1617. The final sermon of the group, dated 1624, was prepared to be preached, but never delivered.

Some of the sermons in the group rank with Andrewes's best work, but others are dull by modern standards, and the group as a whole lacks the richness of the Nativity group and the intensity of the Passion sermons. Perhaps the Resurrection story offers fewer possibilities for the preacher than does the birth or death of Christ. The Resurrection of Christ is not described in the Bible, and the only genuinely interesting incident associated with the event is the appearance of the Risen Lord to Mary Magdalene in the garden, a story which Andrewes fully develops in the best sermon in this series.

As in the other categories, the first sermon provides an introduction to the group as a whole. Here, in his Easter sermon preached in 1606, Andrewes briefly attempts to establish the fact of Christ's Resurrection by referring to various New Testament witnesses. It is in this introductory sermon that the great theme of the Resurrection sermons is presented: the conflict between death and resurrection. The sermon text proclaims the theme: "Knowing that Christ, being raised from the dead, dieth no more; death hath no more dominion over Him" (Romans 6:9). Andrewes states the theme concisely near the beginning of the sermon, noting that it is difficult to disentangle death from life: "The truth is, we cannot speak of rising well without mention of the *terminus a quo*, from whence He rose. By means, whereof these two, 1. Christ's dying, and 2. His rising, are so linked together, and their audits so entangled one with another, as it is very hard to sever them."[1]

The theme of dying and rising is beautifully developed in an unusually fine paragraph:

> This then we know first: that death is not a fall like that of Pharaoh into the sea, that "sunk down like a lump of lead" into the bottom, and never came up more; but a fall like that of Jonas into the sea, who was received by a fish, and after cast up again. It is our Saviour Christ's own simile. A fall, not like that of the Angels into the bottomless pit, there to stay for ever; but like to that of men into their beds, when they make account to stand up again. A fall, not as of a log or stone to the ground, which, where it falleth there it lieth still; but as a wheat-corn into the ground, which is quickened and springeth up again.[2]

This brief passage is constructed on a series of three antitheses illustrating death and rising: from the Bible (Pharaoh and Jonas), from the Chain of Being (Angels and Men), and from the natural world (the log, or stone, and the wheat-corn). The variations and correlations of this passage provide a fine example of Andrewes's art of compressing much matter into little space.

In the next paragraph, Andrewes introduces Mary Magdalene, who appears in many of his Resurrection sermons, and he again presents the dominant theme of death and resurrection: "He that this day did rise, and rising was seen of Mary Magdalene in the likeness of a gardener, this Gardener will look to it, that man shall have his spring." The subject of Mary and the gardener, presented here in embryo, is brilliantly expanded by Andrewes years later, in the climactic sermon in this group.

I *Imagery in the Sermons*

The subject of death and rebirth introduced in the first sermon is the theme of the whole Resurrection group; but the main strength of these sermons lies in the richness of their imagery. As in the Passion sermons, Andrewes's imagery is traditional. He associates the risen Christ with Old Testament types: Joseph, Sampson, Job, Daniel, and, above all, Jonah; and in depicting the theme of resurrection he derives his dominant imagery from the rebirth of Nature. In his introductory sermon, he notes Tertullian's association of Christ's Resurrection with the resurrection of the year; and natural imagery adorns succeeding sermons in the group just as it does the Ash Wednesday sermons. For example, in the sermon preached in 1612 on Christ as Passover, he creates a brief passage aptly blending the Passover of Heaven and earth: "And even nature's Passover, the general Passover is even at this time, both in Heaven and earth. Above in Heaven, where the sun having past over all the signs is come about, and renews his course at the first sign in the Zodiac. And beneath in earth, from the sharp time of winter, and fermenting time of the earth, to the renewing sweet time, the time of the spring, wherein there is *nova conspersio* in nature itself."[3]

Yet surprisingly, the most striking passage on Nature in the whole group, and one of the most memorable paragraphs in any of Andrewes's sermons, depicts not the resurrection of Nature but its decay: "It is now the time of flowers, and from flowers doth the Apostle take his term of *Marcescere*. It is properly the fading of the rose. Straight of itself doth the rose *marcere*, and the violet *livere*, 'wax pale and wan.' Their best, their flourishing estate they hold not long; neither the flowers that are worn, nor they that wear them neither—they, nor we; but decay we do, God wot, in a short time."[4] And it is the imagery of Nature which climaxes Andrewes's greatest sermon in the group, the one on Mary Magdalene.

The imagery of first fruits introduces one of Andrewes's finest passages on the basic Resurrection theme of Christ's exaltation over death. This paragraph from the Easter sermon of 1614, on the text "For this cause hath God also highly exalted him" (Philippians 2:9), provides another example of Andrewes's ability to compress much matter into small compass. Here the simple sentences nicely develop the idea of an upward progression in space:

> This day is the feast of the first fruits. On it, He had no more, but the first-fruits of His exalting. He was exalted, but with Jonah's exaltation only, from the lower parts to the upper parts of the earth. But we shall follow Him higher, to the exaltation of Elias, *super*, "above" the clouds; nay, *super* "above" the stars, above the Heavens, and the Heavens of the Heavens, till we have brought Him from *de profundis*, to *in excelsis*, "from the lowest part of the earth" to "the highest place in Heaven," even to the right hand of God. And higher we cannot go.[5]

In order to emphasize Christ's exaltation, Andrewes frequently presents for contrast striking passages describing the Passion. The imagery derived from the text is frequently expanded into conceits. In his sermon preached in 1611 on the text "The Stone Which the builders refused . . . is become the Head of the corner" (Psalm 118:22), for instance, the Passion is depicted by means of building imagery: "Before they cast Him aside, this poor Stone, they hacked and hewed it, and mangled it piteously; they shewed their malice even in that too. *Caelaverunt sculpturam Ejus*, saith the Prophet, their tools walked on Him, 'they graved Him,' and cut Him with a witness, and made Him full of eyes on every side."[6] This sermon, preached on Easter Sunday, March 24, celebrates both Christ's Resurrection and the eighth anniversary of the king's accession. Near the end of the sermon, Andrewes reveals his ingenuity as he compliments the king while still employing the building imagery of the text. He plays with the Latin words, declaring that the king, since he rules three kingdoms, is not *caput anguli* but *caput trianguli*, and he elaborately compares the fates of Christ and the king. As Christ was confronted by Caiphas, so the king had been attacked by "the High Priest, he that claimeth Caiphas' place." (Probably the pope in the Bellarmine controversy is meant.) As Christ was resurrected from the dead, so the king had been brought back from death's door. Andrewes's subsequent description of the Gunpowder Plot also employs this building imagery.

Four years later, in 1615, in preaching on the text "Dissolve this Temple, and within three days I will raise it up again" (John 2:19), Andrewes again uses building imagery, making an extravagant comparison of Christ's Passion with the destruction of the temple: "For indeed, *solutum est Templum hoc*, this Temple of His body, the Spirit from the flesh, the flesh from the blood was loosed quite. The roof of it, His head, loosed with thorns, the foundation, His feet, with nails. The side aisles as it were, His hands both, likewise. And His body as the body of the Temple, and His heart in the midst of His body as the *Sanctum Sanctorum*, with the spear loosed all."[7]

II *The Resurrection Sermons of 1617 and 1618*

The most extended use of typology occurs in the sermon on the sign of Jonah, preached in 1617 before the king at Durham Cathedral during his progress to Scotland. This sermon is unique both in place of delivery and in method. The text is Jesus' words on the Pharisees, "no sign shall be given . . . save the sign of the Prophet Jonas" (Matthew 12:39), and the sermon is divided into two main sections: an attack on the Pharisees and an extended typological comparison between the *signum* of Jonah in the whale and the *signatum* of Christ in the grave. The sermon is remarkable for the vigor of its language and its ingenuity in developing the typology. In his attack on the Pharisees, Andrewes's voice is humorously ironic: "Well, howsoever they might err that way, the men otherwise to be respected; they were so virtuous men, so straight livers. See ye not their phylacteries, how broad they wear them?"[8] Both parts of the sermon contain colloquialism and wordplay to a greater degree than in any other sermon in the group, characteristics frequently present when Andrewes's emotions are aroused. In attacking the Pharisees, collectively as well as individually, he declares that "the whole bunch was no better," he refers to "their whistling" for a sign, and he asserts that the sign given them was "for their want, not for their wanton desires." The comparison between Jonah and Christ is also embellished with wordplay and rhyme: "Of that history this the mystery"; "the whale's belly that seemed his tomb, proved his womb"; "what is the profit of this sign of the Prophet?"

The bulk of the sermon is an elaborate comparison between Jonah and Christ. The three days Jonah is thrown into the sea correspond to the time of Christ on the cross, Jonah in the whale to Christ in the grave, and Jonah's delivery to Christ's Resurrection. The description of each day ends with an allusion to the days of Creation in the Book of Genesis. There is a concise allegory comparing the world of sinners to a ship's voyage; there are descriptive flashes recalling the Crucifixion and brief passages on Nature's rebirth symbolizing the resurrection of the dead; there is a division of the whale of the text into three: Jonah's whale (danger), Christ's whale (Death), and "that great spiritual Leviathan, Satan"; and there is an elaborate application to the congregation, urging repentance. This whole passage of extended typology provides a full and intricate climax to a sermon unique in Andrewes's work.

On the following Easter, in 1618, Andrewes preached another unusual sermon. The text is "But if any man seem to be contentious, we have no such custom, neither the Churches of God" (I Corinthians 11:16). Andrewes admits that "This is no Easter text," and the sermon is really more like a lecture. The work is the longest in the Resurrection group, extending to twenty-four pages, and it is divided into two main sections: an attack on contentious Christians and a long historical justification of the custom of keeping Easter, with numerous citations from authorities. This last section is overly long and dull, but the first section provides an interesting glimpse of Andrewes as a controversialist, revealing the spirit of the English champion who, years before, had fought Cardinal Bellarmine.

Andrewes's language as a controversialist is confident and robust. In examining the motivation of contentious men his voice is vigorously dramatic, and he also reveals practical insight into human behavior: "Good Lord! Why should any love to be 'contentious?' Why? It is the way to be somebody. In time of peace, what reckoning is there of Wat Tyler, or Jack Straw? Make a sedition, and they will bear a brain with the best."[9] His voice beomes ironic in referring to those of his contemporaries who believe that Easter should not be celebrated at all: "Great pity some in our days had not been then living to have advised the Church to have saved her pains, and never have striven so about it; the shortest way was to have made no more ado, but kept none at all."[10] He enjoys playing with names: "Primianus and Maximianus were the heads of the two factions of Donatists in St. Augustine's time. He saith, it was well for them that faction fell out; else Primianus might have been *Postreminianus*, and Maximianus be *Minimianus*, well enough." And he humorously plays with the name of an early heretic who had been opposed to keeping Easter: "but as Aerius was his name, so was his opinion, and so it vanished into air, and was blown over straight."[11] This controversial sermon is so different from the others in the group that it would be interesting to know if there were any special circumstances which caused it be delivered.

III *Sermons on Mary Magdalene*

Andrewes was commissioned by King James to preach the Easter sermon in 1619 when the king was sick at Royston,[12] but if the sermon was preached, it has not survived. On the next Easter, however, in 1620, Andrewes turned to the subject of Mary Magdalene in the first of three sermons on the text in the Gospel of John describing her meeting with Jesus in the garden after the Resurrection. Throughout his years as a preacher, the Magdalene attracted his attention as she attracted the attention of his age. In an early sermon preached before Queen Elizabeth on Mary's act of love in anointing Jesus' head, he presented a veiled allusion to the queen's devotion to the Church. In his first Resurrection sermon, he followed Augustine in declaring that Mary's resurrection from sin was a greater miracle than her brother Lazarus' resurrection from the dead, a sentiment he repeated, eleven years later, in his sermon on the sign of Jonah. He devoted the Easter sermon of 1608 to the story, from Mark's Gospel, of the women at the sepulcher, noting the precedence given to the Magdalene as the chief of sinners. And in his Ash Wednesday sermon, preached in 1619, he presented

Mary's weeping as an example of penitence in a striking sentence which anticipates the famous poem of Crashaw: "Mary Magdalene wept enough to have made a bath."[13] One year later, on Easter Sunday in 1620, he turns his full attention to the subject.

The three sermons on Mary's meeting with Jesus bring to a climax the Resurrection group as the Wise Men sermons crown the Nativity group. Each of the sermons focuses on a different section of the text: the 1620 sermon on the confrontation between Mary and Jesus, the 1621 sermon on Jesus' command "Touch Me Not," and the 1622 sermon on Jesus' words of commission to Mary. The 1620 sermon, preached the same year as the first Wise Men sermon, is one of Andrewes's greatest achievements. Its chief virtue lies in the singlemindedness with which he focuses the entire sermon on Mary's character. Near the beginning of the sermon he even appears reluctant to make the traditional division of the text, declaring that "if I should divide it, I would make those three parties the three parts; I. Mary Magdalene, II. the Angels, III. and Christ our Saviour. Mary Magdalene begins her part in the first verse, but she goes along through them all."[14] Although Andrewes does develop thoroughly each verse of the text, the real focus of the sermon rests on Mary. Early in the sermon, Andrewes declares he will present ten examples of her love. Not only does he fulfill his promise, but in presenting the last two examples he penetrates to the humanity of the character. In discussing Mary's words to the stranger whom she believes to be the gardener, Andrewes observes how three times she refers to the Christ whom she seeks as "Him," her love causing her to forget that she never names or tells whom she seeks. He also notes how her love blinds her to the fact that, as a weak woman, she would not be able to fetch the body of Christ as she desired. And he declares that her speech "seems rather the speech of a porter, or of some lusty strong fellow at least, than of a silly weak woman" but "love makes women more than women."[15]

The climax of the Gospel story is Mary's recognition of Jesus, and Andrewes sensitively recreates this moment, using a simple image:

> And now, lo Christ is found; found alive, That was sought dead. A cloud may be so thick we shall not see the sun through it. The sun must scatter that cloud, and then we may. Here is an example of it. It is strange a thick cloud of heaviness had so covered her, as see Him she could not through it; this one word, these two syllables, Mary, from His mouth, scatters it all. No sooner had His voice sounded in her ears but it drives away all the

mist, dries up her tears, lightens her eyes, that she knew Him straight, and answers Him with her wonted salutation, "Rabboni."[16]

Andrewes also recreates the setting of the story. Taking a hint from Gregory, he presents Christ in the image of a gardener; and his imagination expands as he develops the natural imagery. It is Christ, the gardener of Nature, who "makes all our gardens green, sends us yearly the spring, and all the herbs and flowers we then gather." At the sermon's climax, it is Christ, the gardener of souls, who brings the dead to life: "For He it is that by virtue of this morning's act shall garden our bodies too, turn all our graves into garden plots; yea shall one day turn land and sea and all into a great garden, and so husband them as they shall in due time bring forth live bodies, even all our bodies alive again." And at the sermon's end, Andrewes returns to the personal level of the text, applying the image to Mary: "The gardener had done His part, made her all green on the sudden."[17]

Like all of Andrewes's best work, this sermon is carefully structured, and it proceeds naturally from Mary to Christ, from seeking to finding, from the grave to the garden, from death to Resurrection, and from the first Easter morning to a vision of eternal life.[18]

At the end of the sermon, Andrewes confides to the congregation that he has run out of time and will not be able to complete his discussion of the text. Perhaps he used the remaining material in preparing the sermons delivered on the same text for the next two Easters. Neither of these sermons is as impressive as the first. The sermon preached in 1621, shifting away from the character of Mary, is an explanation and justification of Christ's strange command, "Touch Me not," with elaborate explanations from Chrysostom, Gregory, and Augustine. The appeal of this sermon is intellectual rather than emotional, and its most impressive passage is actually a digression in which Andrewes vigorously attacks the pride of his contemporaries who ignore Christ's command, "Touch Me not": "Yet are there in the world that make but a shallow of this great deep, they have sounded it to the bottom. God's secret decrees they have them at their fingers' ends, and can tell you the number and the order of them just, with 1, 2, 3, 4, 5. Men that sure must have been in God's cabinet, above the third heaven, where St. Paul never came. Mary Magdalene's touch was nothing to these."[19]

The character of the Magdalene gradually disappears in the 1622 sermon on Christ's words of commission, "but go to My brethren, and say unto them, I ascend unto My Father and your Father, and to My God and your God," and much of the sermon metaphorically depicts the four parts of the text as the four wheels of a chariot. The sermon focuses on Christ's Ascension rather than on His Resurrection, although the most memorable passage utilizes the familar imagery from Nature:

All things in Heaven and earth do so; rising, they ascend presently. In Heaven the stars, they be no sooner risen above the horizon, but they are in their ascendant *eo ipso,* and never leave ascending till they be in the highest point over our heads, in the very top of the sky. In earth, the little spires that peep out of the ground, now at this time, nature's time of her yearly resurrection, they be no sooner out but up they shoot, and never leave to aspire till they have attained the full pitch of their highest growth they can ascend to.[20]

IV *Last Resurrection Sermons*

The sermon preached in 1623 is in sharp contrast to the sermons on Mary Magdalene. It is Andrewes's most powerful Resurrection sermon on Christ's victory over death. The text is a robust passage from the sixty-third chapter of Isaiah: "Who is this that cometh from Edom, with red garments from Bosrah? . . . Wherefore is thine apparel red, and thy garments like him that treadeth in the winepress?" As in all of Andrewes's best sermons, his imagination is highly stimulated by the text; and early in the sermon he eagerly seizes on the allegory: "Go we then to the kernel and let the husk lie; let go the dead letter, and take we to us the spiritual meaning that hath some life in it."[21]

The whole sermon is a vigorous and thorough development of the allegorical possibilities of the text in which the treader of the winepress is Christ, Edom is death, and Bosrah, Hell. It progresses powerfully from an extended contrast of the two winepresses of Christ's Passion and Resurrection to a glimpse, at the sermon's end, of the third winepress of the Day of Judgment. The sermon is strengthened by the vigor of its language and the powerful suggestiveness of its descriptions, the following sentence, from near the beginning, providing a good example: "For He that was led 'as a sheep to be slain,' and so was slain there, He it is and no other That rises and comes here back like a lion 'from Bozrah,' imbrued with blood, the blood of His enemies." And the most powerful passage on Christ's Resurrection in the whole group is the following description of Christ's overcoming death:

"He loosed the pains of hell," trod upon the serpent's head, and all to bruised it, took from death his "sting," from hell his "victory," that is his standard, alluding to the Roman standard that had in it the image of the goddess Victory. Seized upon the *chirographum contra nos,* the ragman roll that made so strong against us; took it, rent it, and so rent "nailed it to His Cross;" made His banner of it, of the law cancelled, hanging at it banner-wise. And having thus "spoiled principalities and powers, He made an open show of them, triumphed over them" in *Semetipso,* "in His own person." . . . and triumphantly came thence with the keys of Edom and Bozrah both, "of hell and of death" both, at His girdle.[22]

The final Resurrection sermon, prepared in 1624 but never preached, is on the famous benediction of Hebrews 13:20, 21. As a whole, the sermon is dull and overly long, but like the last sermons in Andrewes's other groups it provides a formal conclusion, giving the impression that the preacher has said his final words on the Resurrection. Appropriately, this final sermon closes with a passage in which the dominant imagery of Nature is employed to depict the dominant theme of the Resurrection group: "That so, there may be a resurrection of virtue, and good works at Christ's resurrection. That as there is a reviving . . . in the earth, when all and every herbs and flowers are 'brought again from the dead,' so among men good works may come up too, that we be not found fruitless at our bringing back from the dead, in the great Resurrection."[23]

Andrewes's Easter Day sermons provide eighteen variations on the single theme of death and resurrection. As in music, the variations are not equally interesting, but the cumulative effect is impressive. In no other group of sermons does Andrewes develop a single theme with such thoroughness; and it would be difficult to imagine how any preacher could do greater justice to the subject.

CHAPTER 8

Sermons of the Sending of the Holy Ghost

FIFTEEN Pentecost sermons appear in the collected edition. Between 1606 and 1621, Andrewes preached before King James on Pentecost Sundays eight sermons at Greenwich, four at Whitehall, one at Windsor, and one at Holyrood-House in Edinburgh, in 1617, when he accompanied the king on his progress through Scotland. Once again, there is also a sermon (dated 1622) that was prepared to be preached but was never delivered.

I *Theme and Method*

Pentecost is the day devoted to the Third Person of the Trinity, and in the course of the sermons Andrewes discusses the four different appearances of the Holy Ghost recorded in the New Testament: to the disciples, on the day of Pentecost, in the form of wind and tongues of flame (Sermons One and Two); to Christ at His baptism in the form of a dove (Sermon Eight); to the apostles from the breath of Christ (Sermon Nine); and to the Gentiles at Caesarea (Sermon Twelve).

Not only do the Pentecost sermons discuss the Holy Ghost, but they also present Andrewes's most complete definition of the nature of the Trinity. His beliefs are wholly orthodox. He declares in his sermon preached in 1612 that the three parts of the Trinity are a unity: one name and one nature, yet three distinct entities, and that the Holy Ghost is God, proceeding both from the Father and the Son as the breath proceeds from both nostrils. Throughout the sermons, Andrewes notes the close association between Christ and the Holy Ghost. Christ's last act was the giving of His Spirit; and the day of Pentecost celebrates a royal exchange ("felix cambium"). After

Christ in the form of man had ascended to Heaven, God in the form of the Spirit descended to earth; "our flesh is there with God, His spirit here with us."

The Holy Ghost can only be pictured metaphorically, and Andrewes uses the traditional imagery applied to Him in the New Testament. His types are wind, fire, water, and oil, and in the course of the sermons Andrewes develops all four. The most powerful use of wind imagery occurs in his sermon preached in 1616, on a text (John 20:22) describing Christ's breathing on His disciples: "By this puff of breath, was the world blown round about. About came the philosophers, the orators, the emperors. Away went the mists of error, down went the idols and their temples before it."[1] The image of fire appears in the first Pentecost sermon, preached in 1606, describing the descent of the Holy Ghost on the Church and its effect on the disciples: "that the force of fire should shew forth itself in their words; both in the splendour which is the light of knowledge to clear the mist of their darkened understanding, and in the fervour which is the force of spiritual efficacy, to quicken the dulness of their cold and dead affections."[2] These words could be applied to the preacher as well as to the early disciples, and it is not surprising that the Pentecost sermons contain more comments on preaching than any other group.

The Holy Ghost as water is often associated with conduits bearing the gifts of God to men. God's ministers are themselves conduits, while even false ministers may bear the grace of God to others: "and they that by the word, the Sacraments, the keys, are unto other the conduits of grace, to make them fructify in all good works, may well so be, though themselves remain unfruitful, as do the pipes of wood or lead, that by transmitting the water make the garden to bear both herbs and flowers, though themselves never bear any."[3] In his sermon preached in 1621, Andrewes applies the image of water to all three parts of the Trinity: "The Father, the Fountain; the Son, the Cistern; the Holy Ghost the Conduit pipe, or pipes rather, (for they are many) by and through which they are derived down to us."[4] And the image of oil appears in his 1608 sermon to illustrate how the pouring forth of the spirit has thinned through the ages: "No ointment at the skirts or edges of a garment, doth run so fresh and full as on the head and beard, where it was first shed; ever, the farther it goeth, the thinner and thinner the streams be."[5]

The main appeal of the Pentecost sermons is not to the emotions but to the intellect. Andrewes frequently employs the scholastic method of making a point, then raising objections, and finally systematically answering these objections, a technique he also uses in other groups. A good example is provided by his Pentecost sermon preached in 1611, on the text "It is expedient for you that I go away: for if I go not away, the Comforter will not come unto you"(John 16:7). Here Andrewes raises the objection of why it was necessary for Christ to leave the world before the Holy Ghost could descend, and in order to impress the objection on the minds of his congregation he creates one of his most farfetched images: "Are they like two buckets? one cannot go down, unless the other go up?"[6] He then elaborately answers this objection by presenting several reasons. Christ did not remain because this would have been an impeachment to the Holy Ghost's divinity, since He would not have been distinguished from Christ in the great works bestowed on men; it would also have been an impeachment to Christ's equality with the Father since he could not, with the Father, have sent forth the Holy Ghost if He had remained on earth; it would have been an inconvenience to the apostles, since Christ's corporal presence could not go with them on their various missionary ventures; and it would have hindered their spiritual development, since they would not be weaned from Christ's corporal to His spiritual presence. Such elaborate justifications of theological points must have appealed to Andrewes's congregations since he frequently uses this technique in his sermons, but for the modern reader the method resembles hair-splitting.

Although impressive passages are scattered throughout the Pentecost sermons, the group as a whole varies in quality. Some of the sermons are excellent, but others are uninteresting by modern standards. At times, especially in the later sermons, Andrewes even appears to be straining to say something significant about a subject which he has already presented adequately. Perhaps much of the difficulty lies in the subject matter. The only dramatic incident recorded in Scripture in which the Holy Ghost plays a prominent part is his miraculous descent on the disciples at the Day of Pentecost in the form of wind and tongues of flame, a subject which Andrewes develops sufficiently in the first two sermons in the group. After this beginning, he never devotes another sermon to the event, and he turns to subjects in which the Holy Ghost is associated with Christ, such as Christ's baptism and His breathing of the Holy Ghost into His apostles. Andrewes shifts the emphasis from the Third to the Second Person of the Trinity, and the Pentecost sermons become just as Christ-centered as the sermons in his other religious groups.

II *Individual Sermons*

The greatest of the Pentecost sermons, and ranking with Andrewes's best work, is the sermon preached in 1614 on Psalm 68:18: "Thou art gone up on high; Thou hast led captivity captive, and received gifts for men." In the introduction, Andrewes elaborately discusses the traditional fourfold interpretation of Scripture and the sermon provides a good example of the possibilities in developing the spiritual meaning of a text. Andrewes declares that "the text begins with the ascending of Christ, and ends with the descending of the Holy Ghost," but he focuses his attention on Christ, and the sermon seems more appropriate for Ascension Day than for Pentecost. As in all of Andrewes's best sermons, he fully develops the possibilities inherent in the text, and the sermon is filled with powerful descriptive passages.

The first section, which develops the theme of Christ's *ascensus post descensum*, begins with an impressive passage emphasizing the contrast, by expanding the three sections of the text in a series of antitheses: "Christ in His ascendant going up, Christ 'on high' is a good sight. A better sight to see Him so, *tanquam aquila in nubibus*, than *tanquam vermis in pulvere*, 'an eagle in the clouds than a worm in the dust,' as a great while we did. To see 'a cloud to receive Him' than a gravestone to cover Him. Better 'leading captivity' than Himself led captive. Better 'receiving gifts for men' than receiving wrong from them."[7]

The section developing the words "Thou hast led captivity captive" contains a vigorous passage in which Christ is depicted as overcoming His enemies in battle and leading them in triumph:

> so He took the lion. Died a lamb, but rose a lion, and took on like a lion indeed; "broke up the gates of death," and made the gates of brass fly in sunder; trod on the serpent's head and all to bruised it; "came upon him, took from him his armour wherein he trusted, and divided his spoils." . . . Ye see them taken; now, will ye see them led? . . . hell led as one that had lost the victory; "the strength of sin," the law, rent and fastened to his cross, ensign-wise; the serpent's head bruised, borne before Him in triumph, as was Goliath's head by David returning from the victory. And this was His triumph.[8]

This sermon contains more contemporary allusions than any other of Andrewes's sermons, and much of its power lies in the surprising juxtaposition of the triumphant Christ with events from Andrewes's own world. In discussing Christ's ascension as preparing the way for redeemed mankind, Andrewes draws his imagery from contemporary reports of geographical exploration: "They talk of discoveries, and much ado is made of a new passage found out to this or that place: what say you to this discovery *in altum*, this passage into the 'land of the living?' Sure it passes all. And this discovery is here, and upon this discovery there is begun a commerce, or trade of intercourse, between Heaven and us."[9]

In developing the section of the text on Christ's leading captivity captive, Andrewes presents another striking picture from his world. "For all the world as an English ship takes a Turkish galley, wherein are held many Christian captives at the oar. Both are taken, Turks and Christians; both become prisoners to the English ship. The poor souls in the galley, when they see the English ship hath the upper hand are glad, I dare say, so to be taken; they know it will turn to their good, and in the end to their letting go. So was it with us, we were the children of this captivity."[10] Andrewes then presents two more contemporary examples of captivities: the defeated survivors of the Spanish Armada and the prisoners of the Gunpowder Plot:

> In the year 88, the Invincible navy had swallowed us up quick, and made full account to have led us all into captivity. We saw them led like a sort of poor captives round about this isle, sunk and cast away the most part of them, and the rest sent home again with shame. Eight years, since they that had vowed the ruin of us all, and if that had been, the thraldom of this whole land; they were led captives in the literal sense, (we saw them) and brought to a wretched end before our eyes. So He that here did, still can, and still doth "lead captivity captive" for the good of His.[11]

After the splendor of the passages describing Christ's ascension and triumph, the remainder of the sermon is anti-climactic.

The sermon preached the following year, 1615, on Christ's baptism likewise appeals to the mind. It is less exciting than its predecessor, but it does provide a good example of a doctrinal sermon, presenting the significance of baptism, the sacrament especially associated with Pentecost. In raising and answering the question, "Why was Christ baptized?" Andrewes ingeniously endows the waters of Jordan with life: "Take Christ by Himself, as severed from us, and no reason in the world to baptize Him. He needed it not.

Needed it not? Nay, take Him so, Jordan had more need come to Him, than He to Jordan, to be cleansed. *Lavit aquas Ipse, non aquae Ipsum*, 'the waters were baptized by Him, they baptized Him not;' He went into them . . . 'that they which should cleanse us, might by Him first be cleansed.' It is certain; so He received no cleanness, no virtue, but virtue He gave to Jordan, to the waters, to the Sacrament itself."[12]

The most powerful section in the sermon, however, is a digression in which Andrewes attacks the Jesuits, contrasting their violence with the meekness of the dove which appeared over Christ after His baptism: "No dove's eye, fox-eyed they; not silver-white feathers, but partly-coloured; no *gemitus columbae*, but *rugitus ursi*; not the bill or foot of a dove, but the beak and claws of a vulture; no spirit of the olive-branch, but the spirit of the bramble, from whose root went out fire to set all the forest on a flame." Andrewes boldly pictures a grotesque transformation of the Holy Ghost, more appropriate to the spirit of the Jesuits: "Sure, one of the two they must do; either call us down a new-fashioned Holy Ghost, and institute a new baptism . . . or else, make a strange metamorphosis of the old; clap Him on a crooked beak, and stick Him full of eagle's feathers, and force Him to do contrary to that He was wont, and to that His nature is."[13]

The controversial spirit illustrated by this passage and directed against those zealots who disturb the established order of the Church provides a powerful undercurrent to the sermons which follow. In his 1616 sermon on Christ's breathing of the Holy Ghost into His apostles, Andrewes vigorously attacks "the voluntaries of our age, with their taken-on callings. That have no *mitto vos*; unsent, set out of themselves. No *accipite*, no receiving; take it up of their own accords, make themselves what they are; sprinkle their own heads with water, lay their own hands on their own heads, and so take to them which none ever gave them. They be *hypostles*—so doth St. Paul well term them, as it were, the mock–apostles . . . work all to subtraction, to withdraw poor souls, to make them forsake the fellowship, as even then the manner was. This brand hath the Apostle set on them, that we might know them and avoid them."[14]

The next year, 1617, when Andrewes accompanied the king on his progress through Scotland, he preached at Holyrood-House, Edinburgh, on the text "The Spirit of the Lord is upon Me, because He hath anointed Me, that I should preach the Gospel to the poor" (Luke 4:18), and he had strong words for those who preach without authority. He emphasizes to the Scottish prelates in his congregation the importance of submitting to Holy Orders, being ordained by proper authority. And his pointedly ironic words, directed against the rebellious Protestant Scots, reveal contempt for those who preach without the anointing oil of the Holy Spirit:

No; no; the Spirit makes none of these dry missions, sends none of these same *inuncti*, such as have never a feather of the Dove's wing, nor any spark of the fire of this day, not so much as a drop of this ointment. You shall smell them straight that have it; "the myrrh, aloes, and cassia will make you glad." And you shall even as soon find the others. Either they want odour:—anointed I cannot say, but besmeared with some unctuous stuff (go to, be it oil) that gives a glibness to the tongue to talk much and long, but no more scent in it than in a dry stick; no odours in it at all.[15]

The next year, 1618, Andrewes preached on the words "And it shall be in the last days, saith God, I will pour out of My Spirit upon all flesh; and your sons and your daughters shall prophesy, and your young men shall see visions, and your old men shall dream dreams" (Acts 2:17). He warns the congregation that these words were not "a proclamation for liberty of preaching." Certainly women were excluded: "Nay, the she sex, St. Paul took order for that betimes, cut them off with his *nolo mulieres*."[16]And he again pours contempt on the ignorant enthusiasts who, without authority, set themselves up as preachers and prophets:

Nothing else this but a malicious device of the devil, to pour contempt upon this gift. For, indeed, bring it to this once, and what was this day falsely surmised will then be justly affirmed—*musto pleni*, or *cerebro vacui*, whether you will: but *musto pleni*, "drunken" Prophets then indeed; howbeit "not with wine," as Esay saith, but with another as heady a humour, and that doth intoxicate the brain as much as any must or new wine; even of self-conceited ignorance, whereof the world grows too full. But it was no part of Joel's meaning, nor St. Peter's neither, to give way to this phrensy . . . There must be some "sons" and some "servants," to prophesy to, to whom these Prophets may be sent, to whom this prophesy may come. "All flesh" may not be cut out into tongues; some left for ears, some auditors needs. Else a Cyclopian Church will grow upon us, where all were speakers, nobody heard another.[17]

III *Last Sermons*

The last three Pentecost sermons which Andrewes preached are disappointing. In the greatest sermons his imagination is stimulated by the possibilities of the text, but in these last sermons it seems that he has to labor to squeeze some meaning from texts which appear to provide few possibilities. For example, in his 1619 sermon, in preaching on the words "But in every nation he that feareth Him, and worketh righteousness, is accepted with Him" (Acts 10:35), he devotes twenty-three paragraphs (seven pages in the modern text) to a barren development of the words "fearing" and "working." In his sermon preached the next year on the unpromising text "This is that Jesus Christ that came by water and blood" (I John 5:6), he takes twenty-six paragraphs (six pages) to develop the words "water" and "blood." This weak sermon was preached the same year, 1620, as his glorious Resurrection sermon on Mary Magdalene and his impressive first sermon on the Wise Men. Indeed, it was during these years that Andrewes preached his greatest sermons. Perhaps with respect to the Pentecost season he suffered a temporary lapse of inspiration. The last Pentecost sermon which Andrewes preached, in 1621, on the text "Every good thing and every perfect gift is from above" (James 1:17), is more appealing than its two predecessors, and it does contain some imaginative passages, but Andrewes devotes too much space in developing the words "datum" and "donum" from the Vulgate text and in mechanically presenting seven errors arising from misunderstandings of the text.

Andrewes's last Pentecost sermon, composed in 1622 (the same year as the great Wise Men sermon), was never delivered. Like the unpreached final sermons in other groups, this work appears as a kind of a valediction, expressing some of Andrewes's deepest convictions. Here he returns to one of his most cherished themes: the importance of order. The text is the famous passage from the twelfth chapter of First Corinthians describing the gifts of the Spirit and affirming the diversities of gifts, administrations, and operations. Early in the sermon, Andrewes declares that the Holy Spirit descended to establish an order, both in Church and State: "For happy is the government where the Holy Ghost bestoweth the gift, Christ appoints the places, and God effecteth the work, works all in all."[18]

Later, Andrewes eloquently defends the Church of Christ against paganism in one of his most luminous passages on the ideal of the Christian Church: "All our multitude is from unity. All our diversity is from identity. All our divisions from integrity; from 'one and the same' entire 'Spirit.' "[19] Andrewes goes on to discuss the essential difference between the virtuous pagan and the Christian, a theme he had presented before in previous sermons of the Pentecost group.

The heathen man emphasizes his own natural abilities and his habitual morality; he is like the spider weaving a web from himself, a favorite image in the Pentecost sermons. The Christian, however, while not excluding natural abilities, recognizes the importance of divine grace and gifts bestowed by the Holy Spirit.

Andrewes's emotions are aroused when he considers those zealots who bring disorder into the Church:

> Some such there are, no man must say but gifts they have, such as they be; but they care not greatly for troubling themselves with any calling. They are even well without. Hop up and down as grasshoppers, hither and thither, but place they will have none; yet their fingers itch, and they cannot hold them, doing they must be; and if they have got but the fag end of a gift, have at the work; be doing they will of their own heads, uncalled by any so that have right to call; and for default of others even make no more ado, but call themselves, lay their own hands upon their own heads, utterly against Christ's mind and rule . . . Good Lord what the poor Church suffers in this kind![20]

This sermon closes with a strong affirmation of the glory of the Holy Trinity, the whole work providing a fine conclusion to the Pentecost group. Indeed, it expresses so forcefully Andrewes's most deeply felt convictions that it is unfortunate that it was never preached.

CHAPTER 9

Sermons on the Gowrie Conspiracy and the Gunpowder Plot

EIGHTEEN of Andrewes's surviving sermons celebrate King James's deliverance from two attempts on his life: the Gowrie Conspiracy and the Gunpowder Plot. The modern reader may regard these sermons as secular, but they are just as religious as the sermons Andrewes preached on the Christian holy days. Sir John Harington, one of Andrewes's contemporaries, declared that one purpose of Andrewes's preaching was "to raise a joint reverence to God and the Prince, to the spiritual and civil Magistrate, by uniting and not severing them,"[1] and the Gowrie and Gunpowder sermons aptly fulfill this purpose.

I *Sermons on the Gowrie Conspiracy*

The Gowrie Plot took place on August 5, 1600, while James was King of Scotland and less than three years before he became King of England. King James himself provided the official version of what happened on that day.[2] While the king and his party were hunting near Falkland one morning, he was approached by Alexander, the Master of Ruthven, who told him that his elder brother, the Earl of Gowrie, had intercepted a Jesuit in his house; and he urged the king to follow him so that he could question the man. After some hesitation, James and his company rode to Perth, where they were entertained in the castle by Alexander and his brother. At dinner, the king was called away by Alexander and led to an inner room in which stood a mysterious stranger. Here Alexander accused the king of the death of his father and declared that he must die. James objected and the young man, apparently moved by his words, said that he would leave, speak to his brother, and attempt to pacify him. When he returned, however, he again declared that the king must die, and he and the king began to wrestle. James struggled to a window and cried for help, which soon came. The mysterious stranger (an accomplice) ran away, but both Alexander and his brother the earl were killed by James's followers. The citizens of Perth were at first angered by the death of their earl and they surrounded the castle, but when the leading citizens came before the king they were satisfied and the multitude pacified. After James became King of England, this day of his deliverance, August 5, was declared a holy day, as it had been in Scotland.

Eight of Andrewes's Gowrie Day sermons survive, delivered between 1607 and 1623. One sermon was preached at Rumsey, two each at Holdenby and Burleigh, one at the Cathedral Church at Salisbury, and one at Windsor. The sermon dated 1623 was prepared to be preached, but never given. Each of the sermons follows the same pattern, beginning with an introduction, establishing the appropriateness of the text for the day, and dividing the text; extending through an elaborate development of each part of the text; and concluding with an application of the text to the deliverance of the king.

The sacredness of the day is most concisely expressed in the last sermon preached, in 1622, on the text describing Saul's deliverance from David and his men. Near the beginning, Andrewes declares, " 'The King rose up and went his way.' And this our meeting now, in this public solemn manner, is to no other end but to rejoice together in the presence of God, and to render unto Him our anniversary sacrifice of praise and thanks, that *Ecce dies venit*, 'Behold the day is come,' wherein he escaped so fair, and went his way so happily."[3]

Andrewes's interpretation of the events associated with the day of deliverance is, of course, favorable to the king, and he presents the two brothers as extravagant types of wickedness. In the collect established for the day thanks were given for the deliverance of the king "from the wicked designments of those bloodthirsty wretches, the Earl of Gowrie and his brother."[4] And in the course of his sermons Andrewes refers to them as "a couple of treacherous wretches," "two brothers in mischief," "a couple of Absaloms," "two wicked imps," and "bloody wretches." Judas is their brother, and their fate was to be cast "into the fiery furnace, where even now they fry." Andrewes takes it for granted that his congregation is familiar with the details of the plot, and he never extensively describes it. The one detail which he emphasizes most, mentioning it three times, is the marks left on the king's throat, which according to tradition could be seen for days after the struggle. Once, in his 1616 sermon on the attempted assassination of the Persian King Ahasuerus, he does present a brief, vigorous description of the king's struggle with Alexander, addressing his words directly to the king in his congregation: "Ahasuerus was not offered the point of a naked dagger, not taken by the throat, not grasped and tugged with till both lay on the floor. . . . Here was old pulling, and wrestling, and weapons out, and drawing of blood; and a kind of battle fought *dubio Marte* a good while, but at last the victory fell on our side."[5]

The story of the thwarted plot provides the occasion for the full and elaborate development of the basic theme of the group: the inviolability of princes. The exalted conception of monarchy which emerges is in the same spirit found in Andrewes's miscellaneous sermons and in the Lenten sermons he preached before Queen Elizabeth and King James. Twice Andrewes reminds his congregation that even the Hebrew word for king, "Alkum," indicates his special nature since it means "no rising against him." And in his sermon preached in 1610, three months after the assassination of King Henry IV of France, on the appropriate text "Touch not Mine anointed" (I Chronicles 16:22), Andrewes presents the ceremony of anointing as the supreme example of the sovereign's special holiness:

> To hold this name then of *christos Domini*, it is not every ordinary holiness will serve, but a special and extraordinary degree of it above the rest, which they are to participate, and so do from Christ, whose Name they bear, eminent above others that carry not that Name; as if they did in some kind of measure partake *chrisma Christi*, even "such a chrism as wherewith Christ is anointed." And the inference of this point, and the meaning of this style of *dii* and *christi* is, as if He would have us with a kind of analogy as careful in a manner to forbear touching them, as we would be to touch God, or the son of God, Christ Himself.[6]

Shortly after, however, Andrewes declares that "Royal unction gives no grace, but a just title only, *in Regem*, 'to be King;' that is all, and no more. It is the administration to govern, not the gift to govern well." In his sermon preached in 1616, quoting Tertullian, Andrewes again associates the king with God: "Now there is not on earth a person more eminent, nay so eminent as the King. *A Deo Primus*, saith Tertullian, *post Deum secundus;* 'Count not God, he is the very first; count God, and he is the second.' None so high as He."[7]

In the course of these sermons, Andrewes also illustrates the inviolability of sovereignty by presenting biblical kings as types. Saul, the first Hebrew king although God's enemy and tyrant, was yet God's anointed and not to be touched. Ahaseurus, the Persian king, even though a heathen, idolator, and tyrant, was still to be rendered allegiance even by God's people. And the good King David is the type for all succeeding kings: "King David, he is in Scriptures, not *persona Regis* only, 'the person of a King,' but *persona Regum,* 'a person representing all Kings' to come after him; such specially as, with David, serve and worship God in truth. We do safely therefore, what is said to him, apply to them all, since he is the type of them all."[8]

The most interesting of the Gowrie Day sermons is the sermon preached in 1616 on the thwarted assassination of King Ahasuerus, which is powerful in the ironic passages directed against the papists; perceptive in the analysis of the characters of the conspirators, Bigthan and Teresh; and vigorous in the descriptive passages of the struggle between King James and Alexander. By and large, however, the sermons lack vitality. At times it appears that Andrewes has to strain to wring something out of the theme, and he occasionally gives the impression of mechanically working up enthusiasm, as in the following vapid paragraph where he develops the words of the text "The enemy shall not be able to do him violence; the son of wickedness shall not hurt him": "For at the name of 'violence,' at but the mention of 'hurt,' every good heart is moved, and come running in about David to see if any 'hurt.' But there is no 'hurt' done—God be blessed—none done; whatsoever meant, none is done. And he falls, if you mark, no 'violence;' nay, not so much as the least 'hurt.' For they be two, these, 'violence' and 'hurt;' and 'hurt' is the more larger. Any 'violence' done? Nay none. Any hurt at all? Nor that neither. Neither? all is safe then."[9]

The subject of the thwarted plot and the theme of the sanctity of monarchy, perhaps, did not afford sufficient inspiration to stimulate Andrewes's imagination through eight sermons. Gowrie Day did not provide the striking paradoxes of the Nativity, the intensity of the Passion, or the exaltation of the Resurrection and Pentecost seasons; and the Gowrie Day sermons remain the least interesting of any group of Andrewes's works.

II *Sermons of the Gunpowder Treason*

Shortly before midnight on November 4, 1605, the king's men discovered twenty barrels of gunpowder under the Parliament building and the "Gunpowder Treason" was thwarted. The plot, hatched by certain dissatisfied Catholics, had been to blow up the king, queen, prince, lords, and commons, when they assembled for the opening of Parliament on November 5 and to seize control of the government in the confusion which would follow. As a newly elected bishop, Andrewes would have been present, and undoubtedly he too would have died had the plot been successful.

Understandably, Andrewes's imagination was profoundly stimulated by this great deliverance; hence he refers to the Gunpowder Plot in his sermons more than to any other contemporary event. One month after the discovery he recalls the day in his first surviving Nativity sermon in a passage which associates the event with the "seed of Abraham" in the text, recalling the deliverance "from the dangers that daily compass us about, even from this last so great and so fearful, as the like was never imagined before . . . and but for which Seed, *facti essemus sicut Sodoma*, 'We had been even as Sodom,' and perished in the fire, and the powder there laid even blown us up all."[10] In his Resurrection sermon preached in 1606, five months after the discovery, Andrewes depicts the delivery from the plot as a resurrection, elaborately comparing it with the deliverance of Isaac:

> how can we but on this day, the day of the Resurrection, call to mind, and withal render unto God our unfeigned thanks and praise, for our late resurrection . . . He not long since vouchsafed us. Our case was Isaac's case without doubt: there was fire, and instead of a knife, there was powder enough, and we were designed all of us, and even ready, to be sacrificed, even Abraham, Isaac, and all. Certainly if Isaac's were, ours was a kind of resurrection, and we so to acknowledge it. We were as near as he; we were not only within the dominion, but within the verge, nay even within the very gates of death. From thence hath God raised us, and given us this year this similitude of the Resurrection, that we might this day of the resurrection of His Son, present Him with this, in the text, of "rising to a new course of life."[11]

Andrewes is frequently ingenious in applying the imagery of the text to a description of the plot, as in the following passage from the

Resurrection sermon preached on the eighth anniversary of the king's accession. Here, Andrewes directly addresses the king, using the building imagery from the text: "That since your sitting in the seat of this kingdom, some there were, builders one would have taken them to be if he had seen them with their tools in their hands, as if they had been to have laid some foundation; where their meaning was, to undermine, and to cast down foundations and all; yea, to have made a right stone of you, and blown you up among the stones you, and yours without any more ado."[12] And in his attack on the Jesuits, in his Pentecost sermon preached in 1615, he pictures a "new misshapen Holy Ghost" more appropriate to their violence, who "instead of an olive-branch, have a match-light in her beak or a bloody knife."[13]

Soon after the discovery of the plot, Parliament declared that November 5 should be a day of thanksgiving for the delivery of the nation; later, it was decreed that sermons would be preached on anniversary days. Between 1606 and 1618, Andrewes preached on that date ten sermons before the king in the Royal Chapel at Whitehall. Although his contemporaries admired these sermons, modern commentators on Andrewes's work have either ignored or attacked them. Since the group as a whole is impressive, the sermons deserve to be better known. Andrewes's imagination was stimulated by Gunpowder Day, as it was by the great Holy days of the Christian Church, and there is no sign of flagging imagination as there is in the Gowrie Day sermons and even in the Pentecost group.

The first sermon preached on the first anniversary of the plot in 1606 provides a noble introduction to the whole group. It develops the appropriate text, "This is the day which the Lord hath made; let us rejoice and be glad in it" (Psalm 118:24), and near the sermon's beginning Andrewes presents a short, eloquent justification of future commemorations of this special day: "We have therefore well done and upon good warrant, to tread in the same steps, and by law to provide that this day should not die, nor the memorial thereof perish, from ourselves or from our seed; but be consecrated to a perpetual memory, by a yearly acknowledgment to be made of it throughout all generations."[14]

The preacher's voice then shifts dramatically from proclaiming the glory of God's special days to denouncing the extravagant cruelties of the conspirators. And Andrewes's attack on the Jesuits, whom he believed responsible for the plot, is especially powerful in its controlled indignation and its ironic repetitions of the word "holy" which strike like the blows of a hammer: "But this, that this so abominable and desolatory a plot stood 'in the holy place,' this is the pitch of all. For there it stood, and thence it came abroad. Undertaken with a holy oath, bound with the holy Sacrament—that must needs be in 'a holy place,' warranted for a holy act tending to the advancement of a holy religion, and by holy persons called by a most holy name, the name of Jesus."[15]

Much of the strength of the Gunpowder Day sermons lies in the vivid contrast between the horror of what might have happened and the glory of deliverance, a contrast which Andrewes effectively presents in this introductory sermon. In developing his first point, he concisely recreates the horror of the intended destruction: "wherein [were] so much blood as would have made it rain blood, so many baskets of heads, so many pieces of rent bodies cast up and down, and scattered all over the face of the earth."[16] Hyperbolic descriptions such as this frequently appear in the group, and it is interesting to observe the extent to which Andrewes's imagination is stimulated by events which never took place. As the sermon progresses, the emphasis gradually shifts from the imagined horror of destruction to the spirit of exaltation, and the sermon reaches its climax with an elaborate proclamation of joy: "This same joy, that is neither seen nor heard, there is some leaven of malignity in it, He cannot skill of it. He will have it seen in the countenance, heard in the voice; not only preaching, but singing forth His praise. And that not with voices alone but with instruments, and not instruments of the choir alone but instruments of the steeple too, bells and all, that so it may be *Hosanna in altissimis,* in the very 'highest' key we have."[17]

This sermon and the group in general reveal the variety and range of vision which bring distinction to the Nativity group. In the course of the sermons, Andrewes compares the English day of deliverance to the great deliverances of the Jews as recorded in the Bible: the Passover, their rescue from the persecution of Haman, and their release from the Babylonian Captivity. He also draws parallels from his own times, comparing the intended destruction of Gunpowder Day with the carnage of the Saint Bartholomew's Day Massacre of 1572, and paralleling, several times, the English deliverance of 1605 with the great deliverance from the Spanish Armada in 1588, "from the fleet that came to make us no more a people!"

And the imagery employed to describe the plot also reveals the richness found in the Nativity sermons. Andrewes can make use of a strikingly homely image, as in his comparison of the plot to a spider's web: "and all the goodly cobweb, that was so many months in spinning and weaving, comes me a broom, and in a minute snaps it down and destroys it quite, the cobweb and the spider, the plot itself, and the author and all."[18] In depicting the frustration of the plot, he uses the same effective image of the ship wrecked in the haven which he had employed twenty-two years before in his Elizabethan sermon on Lot's wife: "Any wreck is a grief, but no grief to the grief of that wreck that is made even in the very haven's mouth. To go the voyage well and arrive well, and then before the very port to sink and be cast away!"[19] In discussing the unexpected deliverance from the plot, he develops the words "we were like them that dream" by presenting a contrasting image of the false dream: "Nay, there is no more miserable case than of him that dreameth the pleasant ivory dream, and when he awaketh finds it nothing so; dreams he is at a feast, and waketh all hungry; dreams he is rich, and waking finds nothing in his hands."[20]

Andrewes's most extravagant use of imagery occurs in his sermon preached in 1616 on the text "The children are come to birth, and there is not strength to bring forth" (Isaiah 37:3). Much of the sermon is an elaborate, ingenious comparison of the plot with the image of children in the womb. Even the accomplice who prematurely revealed the plot is compared to a woman being delivered before her time. And the most farfetched passage is a two-fold comparison of the plot with the womb and the Trojan horse:

> In imitation of the natural womb wherein we lay, and whence we come all, there is by analogy another artificial, as art doth frame it. Such, I mean, as was the Trojan horse, of which the poet—*Uterumque armato milite complent*, the belly or womb, when it was full of armed men; and so many armed men as there were, so many children, after a sort, might be said to be in it. And if that, may we not affirm as much of the vault or cellar, with as good reason? The verse will hold of it too—*Uterumque nitrato pulvere complent*. The *uterus*, or womb of it, crammed as full with barrels of powder, as was the Trojan horse with men of arms. This odds only: every one of these children, every barrel of powder, as much, nay more force in it to do mischief, than twenty of those in the Trojan horse's belly.[21]

In developing this unusual image, Andrewes even appears to experience a joy of discovery: "The more I think of it, the more points of correspondence do offer themselves to me, of a birth and coming to a birth, and that in every degree." And he then proceeds to develop a ten-fold comparison of the plot with a child in the womb.

Not only does Andrewes's imagination powerfully recreate the imagined destruction and the real deliverance of Gunpowder Day, but it also proceeds from this central event to other related themes. Behind all the sermons lies the theme of "joint reverence to God and Prince" which Harington had found so prominent in Andrewes's preaching. Andrewes devotes an entire sermon preached in 1614 to the text "fear thou the Lord, and the King" (Proverbs 24:21) and in a sermon he preached the preceding year on the text "By Me Kings reign" (Proverbs 8:15), he presented the familiar themes of the sanctity of the Prince and the importance of the well-ordered commonwealth. In presenting the claims of the "spiritual magistrate," Andrewes devotes a portion of the sermon preached in 1616 to a practical discussion of Christian worship, and one of his most fruitful subjects, appearing in some of his most impressive passages, is the theme of the boundless mercies of God.

This is the subject of the most magnificent sermon in the group, preached on the tenth anniversary of the plot in 1615. The text is "The Lord is good to all, and His mercies are over all his works" (Psalm 145:9), and in no other sermon does Andrewes's imagination range so extensively in space and in time. Near the beginning of the sermon he declares that God's mercy is "The super of latitude and expansion, no less than of altitude and elevation," and his imagination expands throughout space as he discovers no part of the universe exempt from the mercies of God: not earth, not heaven, not the small or the large (the ant or the elephant), not even hell itself. His imagination also progresses in time, beginning with the mercies of God revealed at the Earth's creation and effectively climaxing this description with a memorable sentence: "So that His mercy it was that removed that universal defect of nonentity at the first." He continues a discussion of God's mercy as revealed in the creation of Man: "the masterpiece of His works;" and "Count Palatine of the world,' and he expresses the paradox of God's special favor by expanding the Psalmist's question: " 'Lord, what is man, that thou shouldst so regard him,' as to pass by the heavens and all the glorious bodies there, and passing by them, breathe an immortal soul, put thine own image upon a piece of clay?" In discussing the mercy of God's redemption through Christ he employs the image of the pelican, "striking itself to the heart, drawing blood thence, even to the very heartblood, to revive her young ones, when they were dead in sin," and he compresses the life of Christ into one effective sentence: 'For when it brought Him down from Heaven to earth, to such a birth in the 'manger,' such a life in 'contradiction of sinners,' such a 'death on the cross,' it might truly be said then, *Misericordia etiam triumphat de Deo.*[22]

The remainder of the sermon is anticlimactic, as Andrewes shifts from the universal mercies of God to His particular mercies revealed to the English nation on Gunpowder Day, but he does effectively project the magnitude of the intended destruction, applying to the day the "super omnia" of the text:

> And *super omnes*, "over all" it would have gone, not spared any, no degree, high or low: no estate, nobles or commons: no calling, sacred or civil; no sex, King or Queen; no age, King or Prince; no religion, their own or others. This is but *super omnes;* nay, *super omnia* it was too. *Super*, Up with lime and stone and timber, iron, glass, and lead; up with floor, windows, and walls, roof and all. Yet another *super omnia:* all bands of birth, country, allegiance, nature, blood, humanity and Christianity; tread upon them, trample upon them all, tear them all in pieces. Never such a *super omnia* in all senses.[23]

The sermon concludes with one of the most majestic prayers found in any of Andrewes's sermons.

This great sermon on God's mercies belongs not only in any collection of Andrewes's best sermons but also in an anthology of the great sermons of the seventeenth century. And it is, indeed, unfortunate that the Gunpowder Sermons have suffered such neglect, since some of Andrewes's most excellent work lies buried there.

CHAPTER 10

Lancelot Andrewes's Achievement and Reputation

I *The Intellectual Achievement of Andrewes and Hooker*

THE importance of Andrewes's achievement in his own age has been most eloquently proclaimed by T. S. Eliot, who accords him "a place second to none in the history of the formation of the English Church," declaring that "the intellectual achievement and the prose style of Hooker and Andrewes came to complete the structure of the English Church as the philosophy of the thirteenth century crowns the Catholic Church." Eliot also asserts that "if the Church of Elizabeth is worthy of the age of Shakespeare and Jonson, that is because of the work of Hooker and Andrewes."[1]

Hooker and Andrewes were friends, kindred spirits, and founders of the English Church.[2] Hooker's achievement, however, may be more readily gauged than Andrewes's, since he embodied the principles of this Church in the *Laws of Ecclesiastical Polity*, a work which has become a classic of English literature. The bulk of Andrewes's "intellectual achievement," on the other hand, lies buried in his two long Latin works of controversy which, although noted in his own age, have never been translated into English. Nevertheless, Andrewes did proclaim the principles of the English Church in his sermons.

After the religious turbulence of much of the sixteenth century, Anglican apologists not only responded to the challenge of opponents (both Roman Catholic and Puritan), but they also began the more positive task of defining the structure of the English Church. Thus the contribution of Hooker and Andrewes was one of definition; neither of these men was an original thinker, but they did crystalize ideas which had emerged in their age.

It is important to recognize that for both men the English Church was still Catholic; it was not a new creation, but a restoration of the purer form of the old church. Hooker, in the course of his eloquent definition of the Church, at the beginning of the third book of the *Laws*, emphasizes unity with the Catholic Church: "We hope therefore that to reform ourselves if at any time we have done amiss, is not to sever ourselves from the Church we were of before. In the Church we were, and we are so still."[3] Later in his work he speaks of his Church's task as reforming "a decayed estate by reducing it to that perfection from which it hath swerved."[4] Andrewes makes the same assertion in his controversy with Cardinal Bellarmine: "Our religion you miscall modern sectarian opinions. I tell you if they are modern, they are not ours; our appeal is to antiquity . . . We do not innovate; it may be we *renovate* what was customary with those same ancients, but with you has disappeared in novelties."[5] These words provide a concise statement of the position of the English Church: an "appeal to antiquity" and a rejection of novelties.

The essential difference between the English and Roman Catholic churches was not doctrinal; instead, it grew out of the question of the source of the churches' authority for their doctrine. Andrewes succinctly answers this question in a frequently quoted passage from a Latin sermon preached before the king in 1613. Here again his "appeal is to antiquity": "we have one canon of the Scriptures given us by God, two testaments, three creeds, the first four councils, and the fathers of the first five centuries for our rule of religion."[6] Thus the authority of the English Church is derived both from the Scriptures and from the tradition of the early church, a position balanced between the Roman Catholics, who emphasized tradition somewhat more than the Scriptures, and the Puritans, who derived their authority solely from the Scriptures.

In their "appeal to antiquity" both Hooker and Andrewes recognize the authority of "the fathers of the first five centuries." In challenging the Puritans's position on the sole authority of the Scriptures, Hooker emphasizes the benefits of the Fathers in strengthening the Christian, in matters of faith and religion. He declares: "But whom God hath endued with principal gifts to aspire unto knowledge by; whose exercises, labours, and divine studies he hath so blessed that the world for their great and rare skill that way hath them in singular admiration; may we reject even their judgment likewise, as being utterly of no moment? For mine own part, I dare not so lightly esteem of the Church, and of the principal pillars therein."[7] And Andrewes, in his Pentecost sermon preached in 1617 to the king and the Scottish prelates, also eloquently affirms the authority of the Fathers: he declares that the oil of the Holy Ghost falls on many by books (chiefly the Scriptures), "but in a good part also, by the books of the ancient Fathers and lights of the Church, in whom the scent of this ointment was fresh and the temper true."[8] Both Hooker and Andrewes refer to these "pillars" and "lights of the Church" far more than to the more recent scholastic writers, although in constructing their arguments both men frequently use the scholastic method. Andrewes's debt to the Fathers is even greater than Hooker's since they not only provided him with citations of authority but also influenced his prose style.

In their renovation of the Church, while looking back to the purity of antiquity, both Hooker and Andrewes reject those "novelties" which they believed the Roman Catholic Church had introduced. In the same Latin sermon in which Andrewes catalogues his church's ancient authorities, he also rejects the following "novelties" of the Roman Catholic Church: relics, the use of Latin in the liturgy, invocation of saints, communion in one kind, transubstantiation, the papacy, and papal infallibility. Neither Hooker nor Andrewes, however, followed the Puritans in their rejection of all Roman ceremonies. In the fourth book of the *Laws* (devoted to the subject of ceremonies), Hooker laments their rejection and then defends their usefulness: "we are to note, that in every grand or main public duty which God requireth at the hands of the Church, there is, besides that matter and form wherein the essence thereof consisteth, a certain outward fashion whereby the same is in decent sort administered."[9] Andrewes also emphasizes the importance of ceremonies, in his early sermon "Of the Imaginations," preached in 1592, declaring that "without them neither comeliness nor orderly uniformity will be in the Church."[10]

Thus the English Church walked a middle way between the Roman Catholic Church and the Puritans, and nowhere is this balance more evident than in the English form of church service, composed of the three equally important elements of the Word (both the sermon and the reading of Scriptures), Prayer and the Sacrament of the Eucharist. Hooker, in the course of his definition of the Church, traces these three public Christian duties back to the Acts of the Apostles: "instruction, breaking of bread and prayer" (Acts 2:42), and he devotes much of the long fifth book of his *Laws* to a thorough discussion of the English Church's balanced position on these components. Andrewes's most extensive discussion of this subject is found in his "Imaginations" sermon (1592). While both Hooker and Andrewes recognize the importance of the sermon, they reject the position of the Puritans which emphasizes the sermon at the expense of other parts of the service, and they also challenge the Puritans' rejection of set prayers and liturgy. Neither man accepts the Catholic doctrine of transubstantiation, but their emphasis on the importance of the Eucharist makes their service far more sacramental than the Puritans'.

Interestingly, many of Andrewes's sermons are manifestations of the three components of the English Church service. The sermon itself is a proclamation, explanation, and development of the Word; it is accompanied with prayers; and it is frequently climaxed with an invitation to participate in the Sacrament of the Eucharist. Indeed, Andrewes's most eloquent statements on the Eucharist are found not in his controversial writings but in his Nativity sermons, which, in addition to their many other excellences, could be considered sacramental meditations. As a modern biographer of Andrewes has observed in her discussion of these sermons, "Here every sermon ended as the words of man fell silent before the Word."[11]

If Hooker and Andrewes are fathers of the English Church, as posterity has designated them, it was Hooker's task to embody the principles of this church in a formal way in his classic apology, while it was Andrewes's function to illuminate these principles in his sermons. Indeed, it could be justly said that the most impressive monuments to the English Church, besides the devotional poetry of the period, are Hooker's *Ecclesiastical Polity* and the sermons of Andrewes and Donne.

II *The Homiletic Methods of Andrewes and Donne*

Although Hooker and Andrewes were in complete harmony in the principles which they proclaimed, their prose styles were markedly different; and Eliot's reference to their "prose style" (not styles) is puzzling in its implied association. Hooker's typical prose unit is the long, frequently periodic, Ciceronian sentence, while Andrewes favors the brief paragraph composed of short sentences and phrases. Andrewes's prose is, in fact, much closer to that of Donne's whose sermons Eliot contrasts somewhat unfavorably with Andrewes's.

How many of Andrewes's and Donne's sermons Eliot had actually read when he wrote his essay is uncertain. His references to Andrewes's sermons are limited to the Nativity group, and it is quite possible that his reading from both preachers was mostly confined to the two editions of selected sermons which he mentions.[12]

Interestingly, Eliot says nothing about either preacher's use of imagery, and if he had heard the term "metaphysical preaching" he does not use it. Eliot, in fact, says little about Andrewes's prose style and nothing about Donne's. He does find three conspicuous qualities in Andrewes's prose—"ordonnance, or arrangement and structure, precision in the use of words, and relevant intensity"[13]—but he does not develop extensively his comments on any one of these qualities. In his discussion of Andrewes's structure, Eliot quotes a long passage from F. E. Brightman on the structure of Andrewes's *Preces;* his discussion of Andrewes's "precision in the use of words" is limited to his famous metaphor of Andrewes's squeezing the full juice of meaning from words; and instead of defining "relevant intensity," he quotes a few brief descriptive flashes from the famous Wise Men sermon, a passage on the *Verbum Infans,* and one other brief passage. Eliot says nothing at all about Donne's prose, presenting instead only vague generalities about the quality of his religious experience. Something about Donne's sermons is "incommunicable" (a word Eliot borrows from Logan Pearsall Smith); about him "there hangs the shadow of the impure motive," his "experience was not perfectly controlled," and "he lacked spiritual discipline."

Eliot's lack of emphasis on prose style is understandable, since the essential difference between Andrewes's and Donne's sermons lies not so much in their prose styles as in their homiletic methods. And it is on this subject of the two preachers' differing approaches to the same task that Eliot makes his most valuable distinction. He declares that "Andrewes's emotion is purely contemplative . . . wholly evoked by the object of contemplation" and that Donne, in contrast, is "a personality . . . constantly finding an object which shall be adequate to his feelings."[14] This perceptive distinction provides a helpful starting point for a more extensive discussion of each preacher's characteristic method.[15]

If Andrewes's emotion is "purely contemplative," his sermons abundantly reveal that his objects of contemplation are the holy days of the Christian year and the biblical texts commemorating these days. Donne's imagination, however, is stimulated by themes rather than by days, and his "personality" finds the object "adequate to his feelings" perhaps even more in the poetic image than in the biblical text. Andrewes's object of contemplation is never himself, but Donne's "personality" is fascinated by himself, by his world, and by the world to come.

Andrewes's reverence for days and seasons is apparent in all the groups of his sermons commemorating the great Christian holy days. His Nativity sermons display all the facets of the Christmas story, and his Resurrection sermons proclaim both the stories and the theme associated with the day. None of Donne's Christmas sermons, however, with the possible exception of the one on Simeon and the Christ child, focuses on the Christmas story. In fact, if the reader did not know from the headings that these sermons were preached at Christmas, he probably would not even be aware that they are Christmas sermons. The object of Donne's great Easter Day contemplations is not the day but the theme, not so much the Resurrection of Christ as the death and resurrection of the Christian.

Andrewes's devotion to the biblical text is obvious. In most of his sermons, he singlemindedly develops the text piece by piece and word by word. For example, in his sermon preached in 1614 on the text "Behold a virgin shall conceive, and bear a Son, and she shall call His name Immanuel," Andrewes thoroughly expounds each important Latin word in the text: *Ecce, Virgo, Concipiet, pariet, Immanuel;* and it is in this sermon that he performs his famous, elaborate dissection of the word "Immanuel." Donne's method is different. In preaching on the same text, in his Christmas sermon of 1624, his imagination immediately seizes on the concept of the mercy of God (only indirectly suggested by the text); and his beautiful prose-hymn on this subject, beginning "God made Sun and Moon to distinguish seasons" (one of the most famous purple passages in all of Donne's sermons), is essentially a digression from the text, masterfully employing the imagery of seasons to develop its theme.

Andrewes's use of imagery grows naturally out of the text, and he rarely elaborates an image. Eliot quotes a passage in which Andrewes expounds on the word "Saviour" from his text, using four images, none of which he develops: "but sure there is no joy in the world to the joy of a man saved; no joy so great, no news so welcome, and to one ready to perish, in case of a lost man, to hear of one that will save him. In danger of perishing by sickness, to hear of one will make him well again; by sentence of the law, of one with a pardon to save his life; by enemies, of one that will rescue and set him in safety."[16] Donne's use of imagery, however, is often completely independent from the text, and he frequently elaborates his images. For example, the metaphor of life as a prison, in a characteristic passage from Donne's first surviving Easter sermon, preached in 1619, is not found in the text "What Man is he that liveth, and shall not see Death?" (Psalm 89:48). Donne's imagination independently seizes the metaphor and eagerly develops it, even to the point of working in a brief concrete image of contemporary London. And it is not until the final sentence of the paragraph, after the congregation has probably forgotten it, that the text triumphantly reappears:

Wee are all conceived in close Prison; in our Mothers wombes, we are close Prisoners all; when we are borne, we are borne but to the liberty of the house; Prisoners still, though within larger walls; and then all our life is but a going out to the place of Execution, to death. Now was there ever any man seen to sleep in the Cart, between New-gate, and Tyborne? between the Prison, and the place of Execution, does any man sleep? And we sleep all the way; from the womb to the grave we are never throughly awake; but passe on with such dreames, and imagination as these, I may live as well, as another, and why should I dye, rather than another? but awake, and tell me, sayes this text, *Quis homo?* who is that other that thou talkest of? *What man is he that liveth*, and *shall not see death?*[17]

The object of Donne's contemplation is also his own personality or, more accurately, the persona which he creates and which appears so often in his sermons. As an example of Donne's use of the sermon as a "means of self-expression," Eliot quotes a passage (entitled "Imperfect Prayers" in Logan Pearsall Smith's edition) in which Donne catalogues distractions in his private prayers. Perhaps the most striking example of "self-expression" occurs in one of Donne's most dramatic passages, from one of his Lenten sermons, preached in 1622 on the text "The last enemy that shall be destroyed is death" (I Corinthians 15:26). Here, Donne triumphantly envisions his future resurrection:

For as upon my expiration, my transmigration from hence, as soone as my soule enters into Heaven, I shall be able to say to the Angels, I am of the same stuffe as you, spirit, and spirit, and therefore let me stand with you, and looke upon the face of your God, and my God; so at the Resurrection of this body, I shall be able to say to the Angel of the great Councell, the

Son of God, Christ Jesus himselfe, I am of the same stuffe as you, Body and body, Flesh and flesh, and therefore let me sit downe with you, at the right hand of the Father in an everlasting security from this last enemie, who is now destroyed, death.[18]

Andrewes never wrote a passage like this one, and if it is contrasted with a characteristic passage from one of his sermons, the different focuses of these two preachers should be quite clear. In Andrewes's Nativity sermon, preached in 1614 on the text "Behold a Virgin shall conceive . . . and she shall call His name Immanuel," after Andrewes has dissected the word "Immanuel" he puts the pieces back together and elaborately develops the concept of the word: "God with us":

This, this is the great "with us;" for of this follow all the rest. "With us" once thus, and then "with us" in His Oblation on the altar of the Temple; "with us" in His Sacrifice on the altar of the Cross; "with us" in all the virtues and merits of His life; "with us" in the satisfaction and satis-passion both of His death; "with us" in His Resurrection, to raise us up from the earth; "with us" in His Ascension, to exalt us to Heaven; "with us" even then, when He seemed to be taken from us—that day by His Spirit, as this day by His flesh. *Et ecce vobiscum*, and lo, I am true Immanuel "with you" by the love of My manhood; "with you" by the power of My Godhead, still "to the end of the world."[19]

It is a significant question whether the characteristic Donne or the characteristic Andrewes is found in such purple passages as these, or in the long stretches of less exciting prose from which passages like these are extracted. Nevertheless, in these passages, the imaginations of both Donne and Andrewes have obviously been stimulated, but the objects of their contemplation are markedly different. The Donne passage is completely egocentric, while the Andrewes passage is wholly Christocentric. The Donne passage is more dazzling with its highly dramatic speeches of the "I" (the hero of the drama), defying the angels and Christ. But the Andrewes passage achieves its quiet power from the ritualistic cadence of the repeated refrain "with us" and from the cumulative effect of the descriptive flashes focusing on all the significant events from the life of Christ: His birth, life, death, resurrection, and ascension. Indeed, the Andrewes passage nicely illustrates Eliot's description of Andrewes's prose, "which appears to repeat, to stand still, but is nevertheless proceeding in the most deliberate and orderly manner."[20]

Donne's descriptive passage does not grow directly either from the text or from the day on which the text was proclaimed, but Andrewes's passage blossoms naturally, like a flower from its seed, both from the text and from the central occasion of Christmas Day: Immanuel—"God with us." The Donne passage is expansive, soaring with the imagination into the future vision of eternal triumph, while the Andrewes passage is compressed, looking back to the carefully circumscribed past events which the text has foretold and which the day memorializes. Altogether, these two passages provide a convenient distillation of the different characteristics of Donne and Andrewes.

III *Andrewes's Reputation in His Age*

Although Lancelot Andrewes was *Stella Praedicantium* in his own age, his star has never shown so brightly in succeeding generations. One of the first to express enthusiasm for Andrewes's preaching was the Elizabethan writer Thomas Nashe, who relates in his *Have With You to Saffron Walden* (1596) how his friend John Lyly had recommended Andrewes to him, probably when Andrewes was vicar of Saint Giles: "By Doctor *Androwes* own desert and Master Lillies immoderate commending him, by little and little I was drawne on to bee an Auditor of his: since when, whensoever I heard him, I thought it was but hard and scant allowance that was giv'n him, in comparison of the incomparable gifts that were in him."[21] Early in Andrewes's career, then, there were some who gave him "hard and scant allowance."

At the court of King James, where Andrewes won his greatest fame, his style of preaching also found at least one critic, if an anecdote related by John Aubrey is true: "It was a shrewd and severe animadversion of a Scotish Lord, who, when King James asked him how he liked Bp. A's sermon, said that he was learned, but he did play with his Text, as a Jack-an-apes does, who takes up a thing and tosses and playes with it, and then he takes up another, and playes a little with it. Here's a pretty thing, and there's a pretty thing!"[22] This negative criticism is exceptional, however, and in Andrewes's age his distinctive style of preaching soon found followers in such preachers as William Laud, Ralph Brownrig, John Hacket, John Cosin, and Mark Frank.

IV *Changing Taste*

During the course of the seventeenth century, the "metaphysical style" of preaching which Andrewes had employed was gradually abandoned and the distinctive characteristics of his preaching style were rejected. Near the beginning of the century, George Herbert, who had been Andrewes's friend, recommends in his advice to the country parson a simple manner of preaching and rejects the older method which Andrewes had used of thoroughly dividing the sermon text:

> The Parson's Method in handling of a text consists of two parts; first, a plain and evident declaration of the meaning of the text; and secondly, some choice Observations drawn out of the whole text, as it lyes entire, and unbroken in the Scripture it self. This he thinks naturall, and sweet, and grave. Whereas the other way of crumbling a text into small parts, as the Person speaking, or spoken to, the subject, and object, and the like, hath neither in it sweetnesse, nor gravity, nor variety, since the words apart are not Scripture, but a dictionary.[23]

Another of Andrewes's friends, Nicholas Felton, Bishop of Ely, also indicates changing tastes, in commenting unfavorably on Andrewes's style as a model: "I had almost marred my own natural Trot by endeavouring to imitate his artificial Amble."[24]

By the end of the century, Andrewes' and his school were already regarded as old-fashioned. John Aubrey declares of Andrewes that "he had not that smooth way of Oratory, as now."[25] John Evelyn, in an entry in his diary for July 15, 1683, reports that he had heard an old man preach "much after Bp. Andrews's method, full of logical divisions, in short and broken periods, and Latin sentences, now quite out of fashion in the pulpit, which is grown into a far more profitable way of plain and practical discourses."[26] This newer style of preaching is exemplified by the sermons of Robert South and John Tillotson, the most popular preachers of the Restoration. And it is Tillotson's biographer Thomas Birch who, in the eighteenth century, makes the first violent attack on Andrewes's style: "the great corruption of the oratory of the pulpit may be ascrib'd to Dr. Andrews, successively Bishop of Chichester, Ely, and Winchester, whose high reputation on other accounts gave a sanction to the vicious taste introduc'd by him several years before the death of Queen Elizabeth. . . . The pedantry of King James I's court completed the degenerecy of all true eloquence, so that the most applauded preachers of that time are now insupportable."[27] These hostile words accurately reflect the prevailing change of taste in English pulpit oratory in Birch's age, and it is understandable that Andrewes's sermons suffered almost complete neglect in the eighteenth century.

V *Andrewes and the Nineteenth Century*

The true rediscovery of Andrewes's works occurred not in the twentieth but in the nineteenth century, the period which also saw the great collected editions of seventeenth-century sermons. Early in the century Samuel Taylor Coleridge prepared the way by eloquently contrasting the method of the "old divines" with the preachers of his own age:

> If our old divines, in their homiletic expositions of Scripture, wire-drew their text, in the anxiety to evolve out of the words the fulness of the meaning expressed, implied or suggested, our modern preachers have erred more dangerously in the opposite extreme, by making their text a mere theme, or *motto* for their discourse. . . . It was on God's holy word that our Hooker, Donne, Andrewes preached; it was Scripture bread that they divided, according to the needs and seasons. . . . Above all, there is something to my mind at once elevating and soothing in the idea of an order of learned men reading the many works of the wise and great, in many languages, for the purpose of making one book contain the life and virtue of all others.[28]

The nineteenth century also produced the first and only complete edition of Andrewes's works, edited by J. P. Wilson and James Bliss (1841–1854), the first extensive biography of Andrewes, written by Arthur T. Russell (1869), many editions and translations of Andrewes's *Devotions*, and, finally, various critical studies of his work.

VI *Modern Times*

Critical studies of Andrewes's sermons in the twentieth century have been both favorable and unfavorable to his style of preaching, but the attacks have been more severe than those of any previous age. Even at the end of the nineteenth century the hostile judgments of the twentieth century were foreshadowed by Alexander Whyte, who, in the introduction to his edition of Andrewes's *Devotions*, vigorously condemned Andrewes's sermons, declaring that they "bewildered and confused" his brain, and lamenting: "What a pity it is . . . that anything of Andrewes's has been preserved besides his *Devotions*."[29]

Early in the current century, Andrewes's method of dissecting the text was criticized in an essay on "The English Pulpit from Fisher to Donne" by F. E. Hutchinson in the *Cambridge History of English Literature*: "The determination to extract the most possible from the sacred text leads him into over-nice distinctions, till he can only express himself with the help of brackets, and even of brackets within brackets."[30] And William Fraser Mitchell, in his classic study (1932) of metaphysical preaching, after thoroughly analyzing the characteristics of Andrewes and other members of his school, firmly rejects the whole metaphysical movement of preaching by claiming that its "components . . . were not such as were in themselves intrinsically valuable, that the use to which they were put by the 'witty' preachers was not consonant with the great ends of Christian oratory, and, that both the material and methods employed render impossible the cultivation of a prose style suited either to delivery in the pulpit or to give religious discourses in their printed form the dignity of literature."[31]

Interestingly, the most thorough modern study of Andrewes's thought (*Bishop Lancelot Andrewes* by the Jesuit scholar Maurice Reidy) is highly sympathetic to his thought but extremely critical of his style. Perhaps the author speaks for our age when he declares that Andrewes's "style at least as it appears in the written sermon, seals off from us of the present nearly the whole of Andrewes' fine theological thought. . . . His ideas do not sift readily from his taut, concentrated writing, one must, in fact, practically pry his thought from the brittle dress in which he clothed it. . . . The difficult, tangled, almost tortured style renders very hazardous the task of reporting his ideas fairly and precisely."[32] And the last paragraph of Reidy's book attributes Andrewes's neglect in our age to this eccentric style: "Lancelot Andrewes has not lived in his sermons: They died almost with the man himself. Their style, atrocious by modern standards, has entombed a great body of edifying doctrine so deeply in a 'dreary cemetery of literature' that it remains, not a vital force in religious thought, but a cold memorial to the early struggles and growth of the Anglican Church."[33]

These words forcefully represent the negative reactions of the modern age to Andrewes's style, but there have also been sympathetic appraisals. Perhaps the most perceptive analysis of Andrewes's prose is given by Joan Webber in her essay "Celebration of Word and World in Lancelot Andrewes' Style." Webber admits that Andrewes, "the greatest of all the metaphysical preachers, is now little known and less approved,"[34] but her own essay provides an eloquent tribute to Andrewes's stylistic achievement. She compares the compression of Andrewes's style to the work of the Baroque architect Borromini and the expansiveness of Donne's prose to Bernini. She emphasizes Andrewes's sensitivity to language, declaring that for him words "become abstract musical shapes, to be used almost like building blocks in the construction of a sentence with expressive form."[35] Her essay convincingly reveals how Andrewes's distinctive prose style, especially his "stylistic brevity," effectively served him as preacher of God's Word.

The most famous critical estimation of Andrewes's sermons in the twentieth century is given by T. S. Eliot, who is highly laudatory both of Andrewes's style and thought. Eliot's essay "For Lancelot Andrewes" was written in 1926, the three hundredth anniversary of Andrewes's death. For Eliot, Andrewes is "the first great preacher of the English Catholic Church," and his sermons "rank with the finest English prose of their time, of any time."[36] Although this famous essay bestows the highest praise, Eliot was not optimistic about Andrewes's future reputation. He prophesies that "Donne will certainly have always more readers than Andrewes, for the reason that his sermons can be read in detached passages and for the reason that they can be read by those who have no interest in the subject" and declares that "Andrewes will never have many readers in any one generation, and his will never be the immortality of anthologies."[37] The tone of parts of the essay is, in fact, gloomy. Five years before its composition, Eliot had published his famous essay on the Metaphysical Poets, in which he appears almost as an explorer charting out new lands as he enthusiastically places the Metaphysical Poets back into the mainstream of English poetry. The tone of much of the Andrewes essay, however, is anything but exuberant, and Eliot's words sound instead like an orator pronouncing a funeral elegy over the dead, especially when he speaks of removing the remains of Andrewes's reputation "to a last resting place in the dreary cemetery of literature."[38]

VII *Andrewes's Enduring Qualities*

Perhaps the most appropriate question to be asked about Andrewes's reputation at present is whether or not Eliot's gloomy prophecy is true. Have Andrewes's sermons received their "last resting place in the dreary cemetery of literature" and do they deserve such a fate?

Andrewes's chosen medium, the sermon, is the most ephemeral of all literary forms. Whereas plays are born again whenever directors and actors recreate them on the stage, sermons never again spring to life with the vitality they possessed when they were first preached. Their fate has been appropriately described by a modern writer who, in discussing the art of the sermon, declares that "a printed sermon is a pressed flower: all of the color and the fragrance and some of the substance disappear. No sermon can ever be as good in print as it was in speech."[39] Even the first editors of Andrewes's sermons recognized this fact when they offered them to their king and to posterity, and they lamented that his sermons "could not live with all the elegancy which they had upon his tongue." Still they thought "a paper-life better than none."[40]

In Andrewes's time, however, sermons in their "paper-life" had just as much vitality as other forms of printed literature. The two dominant literary forms of his age, plays and sermons, were not only "performed" from stages and pulpits but were also read as popular literature; and sermons continued to be popular forms of literature all through the nineteenth century. It is indeed ironic that Eliot's great praise of Andrewes's achievement came at a period in which sermons for the first time ceased to be read as popular literature. Andrewes's relative neglect in the twentieth century, therefore, is partially bound up with the neglect of the form in which he chose to embody the fruits of his inspiration.

There is no reason, however, why the modern reader who derives pleasure from reading the best plays and poems of the Elizabethan and Jacobean periods should not also enjoy reading the finest sermons from the greatest age of English pulpit oratory. Andrewes's work, like that of other preachers and literary artists, is uneven, but the best of his sermons do provide models of distinguished pulpit oratory and examples of superior literature.

Although Andrewes's distinctive preaching style will never be imitated by preachers in modern times, some of his most basic characteristics still provide appropriate models. Andrewes's awareness of the special disposition of his congregation and his sensitivity to the possibilities of language in conveying the message represent the common challenge and response facing all preachers at all times. Even though few modern preachers would imitate Andrewes's method of wringing every last possible ounce of meaning from the biblical text, many could profitably follow his singleminded devotion to the text as an obvious means of providing a strong foundation for the sermon and as a means also of encouraging unity. Since formlessness is a major fault marring so many contemporary sermons, Andrewes's firm sense of structure could well provide a valuable example to modern preachers. His famous sermon on the Wise Men, in addition to its many other excellences, is beautifully structured, unified by the dominant image of the star, developed from the text. Here all the integrated parts work together, achieving an underlying purpose and building to a powerful, emotional climax.

As literature, also, the best of Andrewes's sermons rank high. His language possesses the vitality found in many of the poems and plays of his age. He shares with the metaphysical poets their sense of organic structure in the integration of the parts into a unified whole; and the strong dramatic voice, which is heard in many of his sermons, modulates in the same manner in which the dramatic voice changes in the typical metaphysical poem. The quality of wit revealed in Andrewes's imagery, always appropriate for the context, adorns his sermons as it does the finest poetry of his age. Andrewes's prose, with its many compressed passages in which the simple, concise sentences and phrases develop and emphasize the theme, provides the best possible example of the typical Senecan style of the early seventeenth century.

Passages and entire sermons of Andrewes rank with the greatest prose of his time. His two brilliant sermons on the Wise Men, his intensely vivid Passion sermons, his sensitive and moving sermons on Lot's wife and Mary Magdalene, his powerful Easter sermon on Christ's resurrection "with red garments," his glorious Pentecost sermon on Christ "gone up on High," and the magnificent Gunpowder Day sermon preached on the tenth anniversary of the plot should all take their places with the finest prose of their age and the greatest sermons in the language.

In one of Andrewes's most personal prayers, he expresses the common desire of his age for a special kind of immortality:

> Grant me the power and the opportunity of welldoing,
> that before the day of my decease
> I may at all adventure effect some good thing,
> whereof the fruit may remain.[41]

The fruits which remain are the sermons of Lancelot Andrewes, and the best of them fully deserve the immortalilty which has already been bestowed on the best work of his time.

Notes and References

Chapter One

1. *The Works of Lancelot Andrewes*, ed. J. P. Wilson and James Bliss, vol. 5: John Buckeridge, *A Sermon Preached at the Funeral of . . . Lancelot, Late Lord Bishop of Winchester* (Oxford: John Henry Parker, 1841; rpt. New York: AMS Press, 1967), p. 287. Hereafter cited as *Works*. References to authors printed in the *Works* will be introduced by the word *Works* and followed by volume number, name of author, title of work, and page number.

2. Besides the biographies of Buckeridge and Isaacson, important biographical facts may be found in the following seventeenth-century works: *The Letters of John Chamberlain* (1597–1626); Sir John Harington, *A Memoir of Bishop Andrewes* (London: 1653, reprinted in Volume 11 of Andrewes's *Works)*; Thomas Fuller, *The Church-History of Britain* (1655); John Hacket, *Life of John Williams* (1692); and John Aubrey, *Brief Lives* (1898).

3. *Works*, vol. 5, Buckeridge, *Funeral Sermon*, p. 289.

4. Buckeridge, p. 289.

5. Buckeridge relates that later in his life Andrewes promoted Dr. Ward to the parsonage at Waltham (although it was more probably his son), and that he kept the picture of Mulcaster "over the door of his study, whereas in all the rest of the house you could scantly see a picture." *Works*, vol. 5, Buckeridge, *Funeral Sermon*, p. 289. Isaacson adds another detail of Andrewes's gratitude to Master Mulcaster, "whom he ever reverently respected during his life in all companies, and placed him ever at the upper end of his table." *Works*, vol. 11, Henry Isaacson, *An Exact Narration of the Life and Death of the Late reverend and learned Prelate and painfull Divine, Lancelot Andrewes, Later Bishop of Winchester*, p. xx. In his will, Andrewes left twenty pounds to Mulcaster's son Peter, although the name recorded in the will is "Muncaster" rather than "Mulcaster." *Works*, vol. 11, *Bishop Andrewes' Will*, p. cii.

6. *Works*, vol. 5, Buckeridge, *Funeral Sermon*, p. 289.

7. John Aubrey, in his "Brief Life" of Andrewes, relates that "Old Mr. Sutton, a very learned man in those dayes, of Blandford St. Maries, Dorset, was his school fellow, and sayd that Lancelot Andrewes was a great long boy of 18 yeares old at least before he went to the University." See John Aubrey, *Brief Lives*, ed. Oliver Lawson Dick (London: Secker and Warburg, 1949; rpt. Ann Arbor: University of Michigan Press, 1957), p. 6. "Old Mr. Sutton" was apparently mistaken, since the records indicate that Andrewes entered Pembroke College in 1571, when he was sixteen years old.

8. *Works,* vol. 5, Buckeridge, *Funeral Sermon,* p. 290.

9. *Works,* vol. 11, Isaacson, *An Exact Narration,* p. v. Andrewes's knowledge of languages was well known in his age. Thomas Fuller declared that Andrewes was "so skilled in all (especially Oriental) languages, that some conceived he might, if then living, almost have served as an INTERPRETER-GENERAL in the *confusion* of Tongues." Thomas Fuller, *The Church History of Britain,* vol. 11, p. 126, cited by Paul A. Welsby in *Lancelot Andrewes* (London: SPCK, 1958), p. 160.

10. *Works,* vol. 11, Isaacson, *An Exact Narration,* p.v.

11. Ibid., p. vi.

12. Ibid.

13. John Jackson, *Epistle Dedicatory* to *The Morall Law Expounded,* cited by Welsby, p. 22.

14. Aubrey, *Brief Lives,* pp. 6–7. Aubrey also mentions criticism which was brought against Andrewes: "But I should have sayd that Andrewes was most extremely spoken against and preached against for offering to assoile or excuse a sleeper in sermon time. But he had learning and witt enough to defend himselfe."

15. Aubrey, p. 6. There is a late account that Andrewes, while at Pembroke, attended Bible studies with Puritans. Samuel Clarke, *Lives of Thirty-two English Divines,* p. 133 cited by Welsby, p. 21.

16. *Works,* vol. 11, Isaacson, *An Exact Narration,* p. vii.

17. *Works,* vol. 5, Buckeridge, *Funeral Sermon,* p. 290.

18. *Works,* vol. 11, Sir John Harington, *A Memoir of Bishop Andrewes,* p. xxxvi.

19. In a letter to Walsingham, Andrewes thanks his patron for the two prebends and dedicates himself: "My prayer to God is that I may not live unworthy of these so honourable dealings, but that in some sort, as His holy wisdom shall appoint, I may prove serviceable to your honour, and to your honour's chief care, this Church of ours." *Works,* vol. 11, *Letters of Bishop Andrewes,* p. xxxix.

20. Harington, pp. xxxvi–xxxvii.

21. *Works,* vol. 11, Isaacson, *An Exact Narration,* p. viii.

22. Cited by Welsby, pp. 56, 57. Welsby presents a thorough account of the debate between Andrewes and Barrow.

23. *Works,* vol. 11, Isaacson, *An Exact Narration,* p. viii.

24. Buckeridge relates: "If it please you to give me leave, I will make his answer for him: *Nolo episcopari, quia nolo alienare,* 'I will not be made a Bishop, because I will not alienate Bishops' lands.' " *Works,* vol. 5, Buckeridge, *Funeral Sermon,* p. 292.

25. John Hacket, *Life of Abp. Williams,* cited in *Works,* vol. 11, p. xviii, n.

26. *Works,* vol. 11, Isaacson, *An Exact Narration,* p. ix.

27. Fuller, *Church History,* vol. 10, pp. 16–17, cited by Welsby, p. 82.

28. *Works,* vol. 11, Isaacson, *An Exact Narration,* p. xxiv.

29. Isaacson, p. ix.

30. Fuller, *Church History*, book 11, cited in *Works*, vol. 11, p. xii, n.

31. John Chamberlain, Andrewes's friend, provides an interesting account of Andrewes's reaction upon this occasion: "I had almost forgot that the bishop of Ely was sworn of the counsaile on Michaelmas day which honor was don him to put him in hart upon the distast he had in missing the bishopricke of Winchester but for ought I heare he is yet as silent as Master Waakes Nuntio the new cardinall." *The Letters of John Chamberlain*, ed. Norman Egbert McClure (Philadelphia: American Philosophical Society, 1939), II, 28.

32. Chamberlain, II, 316.

33. Fuller, *Church History*, book 10, cited in *Works*, vol. 11, p. lvi.

34. *Peter Langtoft's Chronicle*, vol. 1, cited in *Works*, vol. 11, p. lix.

35. Edmund Waller, "Life" in *Poems*, pp. vi–vii, cited by Welsby, p. 202.

36. *Works*, vol. 5, Buckeridge, *Funeral Sermon*, pp. 295–96.

37. Ibid., pp. 296–97.

38. Ibid., p. 298. The most effusive eulogy for Andrewes was made by John Hacket, one of Andrewes's former students: "This is that Andrewes, the ointment of whose name is sweeter than all spices . . . . This is that celebrated Bishop of Winton, whose learning King James admired above all his chaplains; and that King, being of most excellent parts himself, could the better discover what was eminent in another. Indeed, he was the most apostolical and primitive-like divine, in my opinion, that wore a rochet in his age; of a most venerable gravity, and yet most sweet in all commerce, the most devout that ever I saw, when he appeared before God; of such a growth in all kind of learning, that very able clerks were of a low stature to him; *colossus inter icumculas;* full of alms and charity, of which none knew but his Father in secret; a certain patron to scholars of fame and ability, and chiefly to those that never expected it. In the pulpit, a Homer among preachers . . . . I am transported, even as in a rapture, to make this digression; for who could come near the shrine of such a saint, and not offer up a few grains of glory upon it?" *Hacket's Life of Williams*, p. 45, cited in *Works*, vol. 11, pp. xxviii–ix, n.

Shortly after Andrewes's death, Milton, at the age of seventeen, wrote his third Latin Elegy, eulogizing Andrewes. In his dream, the poet sees Andrewes in Paradise, wearing a robe of shining white; the angels applaud as the old man enters Heaven. Later, in his *Reason of Church Government* (1642), Milton speaks unfavorably of the "shallow reasonings" he found in the "rude draughts" of Andrewes's *Summary View of the Government both of the Old and New Testament*.

Crashaw wrote an English poem appearing under John Payne's portrait of Andrewes, prefixed to the collected editions of Andrewes's sermons:

'. . . If you think

Tis but a dead face Art doth heer bequeath,
Look on the following leaves and see him breath.

Crashaw also wrote two other brief poems, in Latin, on Andrewes's portrait.

39. Buckeridge, p. 287.

40. Cited by Welsby, p. 56.

41. *Works*, vol. 5, Buckeridge, pp. 292–93.

42. David Lloyd, *State Worthies from the Reformation to the Revolution*, p. 347, cited by Welsby, p. 228.

43. Buckeridge, p. 296. Apparently Andrewes devoted his mornings entirely to scholarship; and Isaacson, his secretary, reports Andrewes's displeasure at attempts to interrupt his routine: "he kept close at his book, and would not be interrupted by any that came to speak with him, or upon any occasion, public prayer excepted. Insomuch, that he would be so displeased with scholars that attempted to speak with him in a morning, that he would say, 'he doubted they were no true scholars, that came to speak with him before noon.' " Isaacson, p. xxv.

44. Isaacson, pp. xxii–xxiii. Andrewes frequently revealed a quality of playfulness in his relationships with his friends. Aubrey reports, in a delightful anecdote, a trick Andrewes played on Nicholas Fuller, one of his suitors: "The Bishop sent for him, and the poor man was afrayd and knew not what hurt he had donne. Makes him sitt downe to Dinner and, after the Desert, was brought in, in a dish, his Institution and Induction, or the donation of a Prebend; which was his way." Aubrey, p. 7. Interestingly, Andrewes employed the wit of wordplay not only in his sermons, but also in his conversation. His friend Bacon reports that after Andrewes was asked whether or not he believed the Archbishop of Spalatro was a Protestant, Andrewes replied: "Truly I know not: but I think he is a detestant." *Works of Lord Bacon,* vol. I, p. 320, cited by Welsby, p. 159.

45. Izaak Walton, in his *Life of George Herbert,* relates an interesting story of a meeting between Andrewes and Herbert, when Andrewes accompanied King James on his state visit to Cambridge in 1615: "For the learned Bishop, it is observable, that at that time there fell to be a modest debate betwixt them two about predestination, and sanctity of life: of both which the Orator [Herbert] did, not long after, send the Bishop some safe and useful aphorisms, in a long letter, written in Greek; which letter was so remarkable for the language and reason of it, that, after the reading it, the Bishop put it into his bosom, and did often show it to many scholars, both of this and foreign nations; but did always return it back to the place where he first lodged it, and continued it so near his heart till the last day of his life." Cited in *Works,* vol. 11, p. xxii, n.

46. *Works*, vol. 2, *Sermon of the Resurrection* 8, p. 320.

Chapter Two

1. *Works,* vol. 6, *Bishop Andrewes' Judgment of the Lambeth Articles,* pp. 289–300.
2. *Works,* vol. 6, *Censura Censurae D. Barreti De Certitudine Salutis,* pp. 301–305.
3. Ibid., p. 301.
4. It is difficult to understand why an early reader complained of the work's brevity. Sir Dudley Carleton to Sir Thomas Edmondes, June 9, 1609, cited in *Works,* vol. 11, pp. ix–x, n.
5. *The Letters of John Chamberlain,* ed. Norman Egbert McClure (Philadelphia: American Philosophical Society, 1939), I, 264.
6. Ibid., p. 270.
7. *Ambassades de M. de la Boderie en Angleterre depuis les années 1606 jusqu en 1611* (Paris, 1750) vol. 4, p. 271 cited by David Harris Willson in *King James VI and I* (London: Jonathan Cape, 1956), p. 456, n. 8.
8. Cited by Arthur T. Russell in *Memoirs of the Life and Works of the Right Honorable and Right Rev. Father in God Lancelot Andrewes* (Cambridge: J. Palmer, 1860), pp. 206, 207, 208.
9. Translated by Welsby, p. 148.
10. Cited by Russell, pp. 212–13.
11. Ibid., pp. 217-18, 219.
12. *Works,* vol. 7, *Tortura Torti,* p. 443, cited by Welsby, p. 149.
13. *Tortura Torti,* p. 96, translated by Welsby, p. 149.
14. *Ephemerides Isaaci Casauboni,* ed. J. Russell (1850), cited by Welsby, p. 151.
15. Chamberlain, I, 295.
16. Cited by Robert L. Ottley in *Lancelot Andrewes* (London: Methuen and Company, 1894), p. 156.
17. Translated by Welsby, p. 152.
18. Cited by Russell, p. 237.
19. Cited by Welsby, p. 152.
20. Cited by Ottley, p. 171.
21. Cited by Ottley, pp. 171, 172.
22. Translated by Russell, pp. 239–40.
23. Works, vol. 11, *An Answer to the XVIII Chapter of Cardinal Perron's Reply,* p. 24.
24. *Works,* vol. 11, *A Discourse, Written by Doctor Andrewes, Bishop of Ely, Against Second Marriage, After Sentence of Divorce with a former Match,* pp. 106, 107.
25. *Works,* vol. 11 *A Speech in the Star-Chamber, concerning Vows, in the Countess of Shrewsbury's Case,* pp. 97–105.
26. *Works,* vol. 11, *A Speech delivered in the Star-Chamber against the two Judaical opinions of M. Traske,* p. 84.

27. Works, vol. 9, *Reverendi in Christo Patris Lanceloti Episcopi Wintoniensis Responsiones ad Petri Molinaei Epistolas Tres, Una Cum Molinaei Epistolis,* p. 191, translated by Welsby, pp. 181–82.

28. Buckeridge declares: "He was, as all our English world well knows, a singular preacher and a most famous writer. He was so singular a preacher, and so profound a writer, that you will doubt in which he did excel; whose weapons in the mouths of the adversary proved as stones in the teeth of dogs: while they thought to withstand or answer them, they bit the stones and brake their own teeth; and so it is true of him, *Responsa ejus sine responsionibus,* 'His answers were answerless.' " *Works,* vol. 5, Buckeridge, *Funeral Sermon,* p. 291.

Andrewes's reputation as a controversialist was not limited to "our English world." From Venice, it was reported that he was "much reverenced by such learned men in these parts as dare read his books and in that point here are many who give themselves more liberty than in times past which appears by some of these nobility who have been heard this Lent using his arguments and disputing with their preachers at their Church doors." Sir Dudley Carleton to John Chamberlain, February 25, 1614, cited by Welsby, p. 161.

29. *Works,* vol. 11, Sir John Harington, *A Memoir of Bishop Andrewes,* pp. xxxvii–viii.

30. John Jackson, *Epistle Dedicatory* to *the Moral Law Expounded,* cited by Welsby, p. 22.

31. *Works,* vol. 6, *A Pattern of Catechistical Doctrine,* p. 58.

32. Ibid.

33. Ibid., p. 31.

34. Ibid., p. 74.

35. Welsby, pp. 23-29.

36. *Pattern of Catechistical Doctrine,* p. 153.

37. Ibid., pp. 170–71.

38. Ibid., p. 174.

39. Ibid.

40. Ibid., pp. 185–86.

41. *Works,* vol. 11, Richard Drake, *To the Christian Reader,* p. 171.

42. Ibid., pp. 171, 172, 173.

43. *Works,* vol. 11, *A Manual of Directions for the Sick with many Sweet Meditations and Devotions of the R. Reverend Father in God, Lancelot Andrewes,* p. 177. Hereafter all quotations from Andrewes's *Manual* in the text will be followed by the page numbers from volume 11 of the *Works*.

44. *Works,* vol. 11, Richard Drake, *To the Christian Reader,* p. 171.

45. *Works,* vol. 11, *A Coppie of the Forme Used by the Lo: Bishop of Elye in Consecrating the newe Churche Plate of the Cathedrall Church of Worc*[R]., pp. 160–63.

46. Andrewes's chaplain, Christopher Wren, was the father of the famous architect.

47. *Works*, vol. 6, *Bishop Andrewes' Form of Consecration of a Church and Churchyard*, p. 315.

48. *Works*, vol. 4, *Sermon of the Gunpowder Treason* 9, p. 376.

49. *Works*, vol. 5, Buckeridge, *Funeral Sermon*, p. 296.

50. F. E. Brightman, Introduction to *The Private Devotions of Lancelot Andrewes* (London, 1903; rpt. New York: Living Age Books, 1961), p. li.

51. *Works*, vol. 11, Richard Drake, *To the Christian Reader*, p. 233.

52. The inscription reads, "My reverend Friend Bishop Andrews gave me this Booke a little before his death. W: Bath et Welles."

53. *The Private Devotions of Lancelot Andrewes*, ed. and trans. F. E. Brightman (London, 1903; rpt. New York: Living Age Books, 1961), p. 106. Hereafter all quotations from Andrewes's *Private Devotions* in the text will be followed by the page numbers from the Brightman edition.

54. The five lines of Andrewes's prose-poem are derived from the following five scriptural passages: Psalm 136:25, Psalm 147:9, Genesis 48:15, Acts 14:17, Hebrews 13:9.

55. *Works*, vol. 1, *Sermon of the Nativity* 10, p. 159.

56. Alexander Whyte, *Lancelot Andrewes and His Private Devotions*, 2nd ed. (Edinburgh and London, 1896), p. 12.

57. When one recalls Andrewes's moral lapse in the Essex divorce case, however, it is tempting to see special significance in his prayer for deliverance from "making gods of kings" (p. 243).

58. F. E. Brightman, Introduction to *The Private Devotions*, p. lxi.

Chapter Three

1. *Works*, vol. 11, Isaacson, *An Exact Narration*, p. xxvi.
2. *Works*, vol. 1, *Sermon of Repentance and Fasting* 7, p. 421.
3. *Works*, vol. 4, *Sermon of the Gunpowder Treason* 9, p. 377.
4. *Sermon of the Gunpowder Treason*, 9, p. 377.
5. *Works*, vol. 5, *A Sermon . . . Of the Doing of the Word*, pp. 186–87.
6. Ibid., p. 198.
7. *Works*, vol. 3, *Sermon of the Sending of the Holy Ghost* 2, p. 141.
8. Ibid., p. 131.
9. *Works*, vol. 1, *Sermon of Repentance and Fasting* 7, p. 423.
10. *Works*, vol. 6, *A Pattern of Catechistical Doctrine*, p. 197.
11. Ibid., p. 196.
12. British Museum, Lansdowne MSS., ccxxxiii, f. 4, cited by Maurice F. Reidy, S.J., in *Bishop Lancelot Andrewes* (Chicago: Loyola University Press, 1955), p. 66.
13. *Works*, vol. 3, *Sermon of the Sending of the Holy Ghost* 10, pp. 280-81.
14. *Works*, vol. 2, *Sermon of the Sending of the Holy Ghost* 7, pp. 222–23.
15. *Works*, vol. 2, *Sermon of the Resurrection* 7, p. 303.

16. *Works,* vol. 3, *Sermon of the Resurrection* 17, p. 63.
17. *Works,* vol. 2, *Sermon of the Resurrection* 12, p. 388.
18. *Works,* vol. 3, *Sermon of the Sending of the Holy Ghost* 10, p. 290.
19. *Works,* vol. 5, *Of the Worshipping of Imaginations,* p. 62.
20. *Works,* vol. 1, *Sermon of the Nativity* 14, p. 245.
21. *Works,* vol. 1, *Sermon of Repentance and Fasting* 1, p. 310. Andrewes had also quoted from this Aeschylus passage in his *Catechism. Works,* vol. 6, *A Pattern of Catechistical Doctrine,* p. 30.
22. *Works,* vol. 2, *Sermon of the Passion* 3, p. 172.
23. *Works,* vol. 6, *A Pattern of Catechistical Doctrine,* pp. 59-60.
24. *Works,* vol. 3, *Sermon of the Sending of the Holy Ghost* 10, p. 287.
25. *Works,* vol. 2, *Sermon of the Resurrection* 9, pp. 237–38.
26. *Works,* vol. 2, *Sermon of the Passion* 3, p. 178.
27. T. S. Eliot, *Selected Essays* (New York: Harcourt, Brace and Company, 1932; rpt. 1950), p. 305.
28. John Selden, the orientalist, reports: "The Proverbs of several Nations were much studied by bishop *Andrews,* and the reason he gave, was, Because by them he knew the minds of several Nations." John Selden, *Table Talk* (1689), p. 49, cited by G. M. Story, Introduction to *Lancelot Andrewes: Sermons* (Oxford: Clarendon Press, 1967), p. xxxiv, n.
29. *Works,* vol. 2, *Sermon Preached in Lent* 4, p. 61. Andrewes repeated this simile, word for word, in his Gunpowder Day Sermon on the text, "By Me Kings Reign" (Proverbs 8:15). *Works,* vol. 4, *Sermon of the Gunpowder Treason* 5, p. 278.
30. Eliot, p. 306.
31. *Works,* vol. 2 *Sermon of the Resurrection* 8, p. 310.
32. *Works,* vol. 1, *Sermon of the Nativity* 1, p. 5,
33. *Works,* vol. 1, *Sermon of the Nativity* 6, p. 92.
34. *Works,* vol. 4, *Sermon of the Gunpowder Treason* 7, p. 321.
35. *Works,* vol. 1, *Sermon of the Nativity* 13, p. 228.
36. Eliot, p. 302.
37. *Works,* vol. 1, *Sermon of the Nativity* 3, p. 35.
38. Eliot, p. 302.
39. Ibid., pp. 308–309.
40. *Works,* vol. 1, *Sermon of the Nativity* 1, p. 3.
41. *Works,* vol. 2, *Sermon of the Resurrection* 3, p. 227.
42. *Works,* vol. 3, *Sermon of the Resurrection* 15, p. 25.
43. Although Charles I apparently never heard Andrewes preach, he must have admired his sermons. Welsby (p. 263) relates that Charles, on the eve of his execution, included Andrewes's Sermons among the books which he recommended to Princess Elizabeth, but Welsby gives no source for this interesting incident.
44. *Works,* vol. 11, Isaacson, *An Exact Narration,* p. xxvi. Before this first collected edition, individual sermons of Andrewes had been published

in the following years: 1589, 1604, 1606, 1609, 1610, 1611, 1614, 1617, and 1620.

45. *Works*, vol. 11, *Letters of Bishop Andrewes*, Letter 1: To Sir Francis Walsingham, p. xxxix.

46. *Works*, vol. 5 Buckeridge, *Funeral Sermon*, p. 295. The whole passage, from which this quotation is drawn, provides a glimpse of Andrewes's dedication in preparing his sermons: "He was always a diligent and painful preacher . . . and he ever misliked often and loose preaching without study of antiquity, and he would be bold with himself and say, when he preached twice a day at St. Giles', he prated once."

47. *Epistle Dedicatorie: To His Most Sacred Majestie Charles* to *XCVI Sermons by the Right, Honorable, and Reverend Father in God, Lancelot Andrewes* (London: Printed by George Miller, 1629), sig. A2.

48. Besides the ninety-six English sermons in the collected edition, seven of Andrewes's Latin sermons survive. There are also three groups of English sermons attributed to Andrewes but not found in the first collected edition:

1. *Seven Sermons Upon the Temptation of Christ in the Wilderness* (published in London, in 1592, with no name on the title page; republished in 1627, a year after Andrewes's death, with Andrewes's name on the title page; and republished again, in 1642, with *The Moral Law* [Andrewes's *Catechism*]).
2. *Nineteen Sermons concerning Prayer* (published in London, in 1611, with no name on the title page; republished in 1641, with Andrewes's name on the title page; and republished again, in 1642, with *The Moral Law Expounded*).
3. *Aposmatia sacra: or a collection of posthumous and orphan lectures: delivered at St. Pauls and St. Giles his Church* (published in 1657; attributed to Andrewes).

It is not completely certain whether these English sermons are Andrewes's works, but they are quite different stylistically from the authentic sermons in the early collected editions. I believe that the ninety-six sermons give an ample picture of Andrewes's preaching style, and I have therefore confined my attention to them in the following chapters.

Chapter Four

1. *Works*, vol. 5, *A Sermon preached at the Spittle*, p. 22.
2. Ibid., p. 13.
3. Ibid., p. 42.
4. Ibid., p. 53.
5. *Works*, vol. 5, *Of the Worshipping of Imaginations*, p. 64.
6. *Works*, vol. 5, *Of the Lawfulness and Form of Swearing*, p. 77.
7. *Works*, vol. 5, *Of the Giving Caesar his Due*, pp. 136, 132–33, 139–40.

8. *Works,* vol. 5, *A Sermon preached on the Coronation-day,* pp. 183, 184.

9. *Works,* vol. 2, *Sermon Preached in Lent* 1, p. 11.

10. *Works,* vol. 2, *Sermon Preached in Lent* 2, pp. 20, 21, 22, 26, 32.

11. Works, vol. 11, Sir John Harington, *A Memoir of Bishop Andrewes,* p. xxxvii.

12. *Works,* vol. 2, *Sermon Preached in Lent* 3, p. 56. Andrewes preached this sermon on March 30, the day before Barrow and Greenwood, the Separatists, were scheduled to be hanged at Tyburn for sedition against the Crown. They were reprieved, but hanged on April 6. Andrewes had held a long discussion with Barrow in Fleet Prison three years before. In the following passage from the sermon, Andrewes draws a parallel between the contemporary event and the Gospel story: "For all the world, as some in our time that sought help of authority, while they had hope that way to prevail; but when that came not, since begin to hold they will and may do it without stay for authority, and seek to subvert the state they cannot form to their fancy. My hope is and so is my prayer, that those which have hitherto been carried with their plots and pretences, now they be informed and see what the truth is, may do as the Disciples, leave Judas in his murmuring, and let Mary Magdalene be quiet." *Works,* vol. 2, *Sermon Preached in Lent* 3, p. 44, cited by Welsby, p. 58.

13. *Sermon Preached in Lent* 3, p. 42.

14. *Works,* vol. 2, *Sermon Preached in Lent* 4, p. 67.

15. Ibid., pp. 68–69.

16. Smith is described as "silver tongu'd" in Thomas Nashe's *Pierce Penilesse*. Nashe attributes Smith's successful preaching to the fact that he had purified his mind with "sweete Poetrie" before he turned to theology. And Nashe declares, "If a simple mans censure may be admitted to speake in such an open Theater of opinion, I never saw abundant reading better mixt with delight, or sentences which no man can challenge of prophane affectation sounding more melodious to the eare or piercing more deepe to the heart." *The Works of Thomas Nashe,* ed. Ronald B. McKerrow (Oxford, 1904; rpt. Oxford: Basil Blackwell, 1958), I, 192–93. Thomas Fuller also describes Smith's popularity, declaring that he was "commonly called the *Silver-tongued preacher,* and that was but one metal below St. Chrysostom."Fuller also reports that the church was so crowded when Smith preached that "persons of good quality brought their own pews with them, I mean their legs, to stand thereupon in the alleys" and that Smith "held the rudder of their affections in his hands, so that he could steer them whither he was pleased." Cited by George Philip Krapp in *The Rise of English Literary Prose* (1915; rpt. New York: Frederick Ungar Publishing Company, 1963), pp. 196–97.

17. Henry Smith, *A Looking Glasse for Drunkards* in *The Sermons of Master Henrie Smith* (London: Printed by Thomas Orwin for Thomas Man, 1592), p. 604.

18. The nature of Smith's congregation at Saint Clement Danes may partially be determined from a petition signed by his parishioners. His congregation contained a grocer, a locksmith, smiths, tailors, saddlers, hosiers, haberdashers, glaziers, and cutters. In signing the petition, many of them signed by making their marks. Cited by William Haller in *The Rise of Puritanism* (New York: Columbia University Press, 1938; rpt. New York: Harper Torchbooks, 1957), p. 29.

19. Gabriel Harvey, "Against Thomas Nash," in *Elizabethan Critical Essays*, ed. G. Gregory Smith (London, 1904; rpt. London: Oxford University Press, 1959), II, 281.

20. Cited by Krapp, pp. 198–99.

21. *The Sermons of Master Henrie Smith*, p. 661.

22. *Works*, vol. 2, *Sermon Preached in Lent* 1, p. 7.

Chapter Five

1. *Works*, vol. 4, *Sermon of the Gunpowder Treason* 1, p. 204.

2. *Works*, vol. 1, *Sermon of the Nativity* 9, p. 142.

3. *Works*, vol. 1, *Sermon of the Nativity* 12, p. 198.

4. *Works*, vol. 1, *Sermon of the Nativity* 1, pp. 4–5.

5. T. S. Eliot, *Selected Essays* (New York: Harcourt, Brace and Company, 1932; rpt. 1950), p. 302.

6. *Works*, vol. 1, *Sermon of the Nativity* 6, p. 92.

7. *Works*, vol. 1, *Sermon of the Nativity* 2, p. 22.

8. *Works*, vol. 1, *Sermon of the Nativity* 4, p. 52.

9. *Works*, vol. 1, *Sermon of the Nativity* 7, pp. 112, 113, 116.

10. *Works*, vol. 1, *Sermon of the Nativity* 6, p. 88.

11. This sermon was especially popular both with the court and the king. John Chamberlain wrote to Dudley Carleton: "The bishop of Ely preached at court on Christmas day with great applause, being not only *sui similis*, but more than himself by the report of the King and all his auditors." Later, in a letter to Sir Ralph Winwood, Chamberlain again praised the sermon: "I hope we shall have his sermon upon the 4th to the Galatians 4th verse, preached on Christmas day last with great applause: the King with much importunitie had the copie delivered him on Tewsday last before his going toward Roiston, and sayes he will lay yt still under his pillow." *The Letters of John Chamberlain*, ed. Norman Egbert McClure (Philadelphia: American Philosophical Society, 1939), I, 292, 295.

12. *Works*, vol. 1, *Sermon of the Nativity* 9, pp. 144–45, 146.

13. *Works*, vol. 1, *Sermon of the Nativity* 11, pp. 181, 187.

14. Chamberlain, II, 130.

15. *Works*, vol. 1, *Sermon of the Nativity* 12, pp. 201–202.

16. Ibid., p. 201.

17. Ibid., p. 204.

18. Ibid., p. 210.

19. Ibid., p. 213.
20. *Works,* vol. 1, *Sermon of the Nativity* 13, pp. 216–17, 220.
21. Ibid., pp. 231–32.
22. *Works,* vol. 1, *Sermon of the Nativity,* 14, p. 245.
23. Ibid., p. 246.
24. Ibid., p. 247. Interestingly, according to a description, in Andrewes's chapel there was "on top of the cover, of the chalice, the wise man's star." *Works,* vol. 11, *Bishop Andrewes's Chapel,* p. xcvii.
25. *Works,* vol. 1, *Sermon of the Nativity* 15, p. 257.
26. Ibid., p. 260.
27. Ibid., p. 258.
28. Ibid., p. 260.
29. Ibid., p. 264.
30. *Works,* vol. 1, *Sermon of the Nativity* 16, p. 276.
31. Ibid., pp. 276–77.

Chapter Six

1. This sermon has been incorrectly dated 1598; it was, however, preached in 1589 and is Andrewes's first surviving court sermon.
2. *Works,* vol. 1, *Sermon of Repentance and Fasting* 7, p. 423.
3. *Works,* vol. 1, *Sermon of Repentance and Fasting* 2, p. 321.
4. Ibid., p. 330.
5. *Works,* vol. 1, *Sermon of Repentance and Fasting* 5, p. 390.
6. *Works,* vol. 1, *Sermon of Repentance and Fasting* 6, pp. 406, 407, 411.
7. Ibid., p. 355.
8. *Works,* vol. 1, *Sermon of Repentance and Fasting* 4, p. 357.
9. *Works,* vol. 1, *Sermon of Repentance and Fasting* 7, p. 428.
10. Ibid., p. 432.
11. *Works,* vol. 2, *Sermon of the Passion* 1, p. 120.
12. *Works,* vol. 2, *Sermon of the Passion* 3, p. 178.
13. Joan Webber, "Celebration of Word and World in Lancelot Andrewes' Style," *Journal of English and Germanic Philology* 64 (1965), rpt. in Stanley E. Fish, ed., *Seventeenth-Century Prose: Modern Essays in Criticism* (New York: Oxford Press, 1971), pp. 341–42.
14. *Works,* vol. 2, *Sermon of the Passion* 1, p. 122.
15. Ibid., p. 126.
16. *Works,* vol. 2, *Sermon of the Passion* 2, p. 143.
17. *Works,* vol. 2, *Sermon of the Passion* 3, p. 173.
18. *Works,* vol. 2, *Sermon of the Passion* 1, p. 120.

19. *Works*, vol. 2, *Sermon of the Passion* 3, p. 180. John Fisher, early in the sixteenth century, had used this image of *Liber Charitatis* in one of his English sermons.

20. *Sermon of the Passion* 3, pp. 176, 177.

21. *Sermon of the Passion* 3, p. 166.

Chapter Seven

1. *Works*, vol. 2, *Sermon of the Resurrection* 1, p. 195.
2. *Sermon of the Resurrecton* 1, p. 192.
3. *Works*, vol. 2, *Sermon of the Resurrection* 7, p. 307.
4. *Works*, vol. 2, *Sermon of the Resurrection* 11, p. 378.
5. *Works*, vol. 2, *Sermon of the Resurrection* 9, p. 329.
6. *Works*, vol. 2, *Sermon of the Resurrection* 6, p. 277.
7. *Works*, vol. 2, *Sermon of the Resurrection* 10, p. 355.
8. *Works*, vol. 2, *Sermon of the Resurrection* 12, p. 387.
9. *Works*, vol. 2, *Sermon of the Resurrection* 13, p. 408.
10. Ibid., pp. 415–16.
11. Ibid., pp. 408, 416.
12. " . . . But the phisicians wish him [the King] not to stir or remove for eight or ten dayes, so that he kepes his Easter at Roiston and thither the bishop of Winchester was sent for and went yesterday to preach to morow." *The Letters of John Chamberlain*, ed. Norman Egbert McClure (Philadelphia: American Philosophical Society, 1939), II, 25.
13. *Works*, vol. 1, *Sermon of Repentance and Fasting* 4, p. 369. Like others of his age, Andrewes identified the Magdalene with the unnamed weeping woman of Luke's Gospel and with Mary the sister of Lazarus.
14. *Works*, vol. 3, *Sermon of the Resurrection* 14, p. 5.
15. Ibid., p. 19.
16. Ibid., p. 20.
17. Ibid., pp. 15, 16, 21.
18. In this sermon on death and resurrection, Andrewes makes one of his rare contemporary references, in his graceful allusion to the queen's death the previous year: "So, no weeping, no being sad; now, nothing this day, but peace and joy; they do properly belong to this feast. And this I note the more willingly now this year, because the last Easter we could not so well have noted it. Some wept then; all were sad, little joy there was, and there was a *quid*, a good cause for it. But blessed be God That hath now sent us a more kindly Easter, of this, by taking away the cause of our sorrow then, that we may preach of *Quid ploras?*" *Sermon of the Resurrection* 14, p. 18. This sermon was also popular with the court and the king. John Chamberlain wrote to Sir Dudley Carleton: "I have sent you . . . a sermon of the bishop of Winchesters which he preached on Easterday last to the Lords and rest of the houshold at court, which was so much com-

mended that the King would needs have him set yt out [publish it]." Chamberlain, II, 309.

19. *Works*, vol. 3, *Sermon of the Resurrection* 15, p. 32.
20. *Works*, vol. 3, *Sermon of the Resurrection* 16, p. 48.
21. *Works*, vol. 3, *Sermon of the Resurrection* 17, p. 63.
22. Ibid., p. 66.
23. *Works*, vol. 3, *Sermon of the Resurrection* 18, pp. 102–103.

Chapter Eight

1. *Works*, vol. 3, *Sermon of the Sending of the Holy Ghost* 9, p. 268.
2. *Works*, vol. 3, *Sermon of the Sending of the Holy Ghost* 1, p. 124.
3. *Works*, vol. 3, *Sermon of the Sending of the Holy Ghost* 9, p. 278.
4. *Works*, vol. 3, *Sermon of the Sending of the Holy Ghost* 14, p. 362.
5. *Works*, vol. 3, *Sermon of the Sending of the Holy Ghost* 2, p. 136.
6. *Works*, vol. 3, *Sermon of the Sending of the Holy Ghost* 4, p. 171.
7. *Works*, vol. 3, *Sermon of the Sending of the Holy Ghost* 7, p. 223.
8. Ibid., p. 229.
9. Ibid., p. 226.
10. Ibid., p. 230.
11. Ibid., pp. 230–31.
12. *Works*, vol. 3, *Sermon of the Sending of the Holy Ghost* 8, pp. 245–46.
13. Ibid., pp. 254–55.
14. *Works*, vol. 3, *Sermon of the Sending of the Holy Ghost* 9, p. 273.
15. *Works*, vol. 3, *Sermon of the Sending of the Holy Ghost* 10, p. 288.
16. *Works*, vol. 3, *Sermon of the Sending of the Holy Ghost* 11, p. 313.
17. Ibid., pp. 313–14.
18. *Works*, vol. 3, *Sermon of the Sending of the Holy Ghost* 15, p. 379.
19. Ibid., p. 385.
20. Ibid., p. 396.

Chapter Nine

1. *Works*, vol. 11, Sir John Harington, *A Memoir of Bishop Andrewes*, p. xxxvii.

2. The king's version of the story is thoroughly presented by David Harris Willson in *King James VI and I* (London: Jonathan Cape, 1956), pp. 126–29. Willson is skeptical and presents some interesting alternatives. There is also a very late tradition recording Andrewes's own suspicion about the details of the plot. It is said that Andrewes "fell down upon his knees before King James, and besought his majesty to spare his customary pains upon that day, that he might not mock God unless the thing were true. The King replied, Those people were much to blame who would never believe a treason unless their Prince were actually murdered; but did assure

him on the faith of a Christian and upon the word of a King, their treasonable attempt against him were too true." T. Plume, *Account of the Life and Death of John Hacket* (1865), p. 21, cited by Paul A. Welsby in *Lancelot Andrewes* (London: SPCK, 1958), p. 142.

3. Works, vol. 4, *Sermon of the Conspiracy of the Gowries* 7, p. 154. In a letter to Sir Dudley Carleton, John Chamberlain provides an interesting account of Andrewes's physical condition on the day on which this sermon was preached: "I stayed somwhat the longer upon notice that the bishop of Winchester was to preach at Windsor the 5th of August, which he did, taking his text from the 4th to the end of the 7th verse of the 24th chapter of the firste booke of Samuell: his voyce growes very low, but otherwise he did extraordinarie well and like himself. I dined with him that day, and could not leave him till halfe an howre after sixe a clocke. The weather was very hot and he so faint and wet that he was faine to go to bed for some little time after he came out of the pulpit." *The Letters of John Chamberlain*, ed. Norman Egbert McClure (Philadelphia: American Philosophical Society, 1939), II, 448.

4. Cited by Welsby, p. 141.

5. *Works*, vol. 4, *Sermon of the Conspiracy of the Gowries* 6, pp. 148, 149.

6. *Works*, vol. 4, *Sermon of the Conspiracy of the Gowries* 3, p. 56.

7. *Works*, vol. 4, *Sermon of the Conspiracy of the Gowries* 6, p. 131.

8. *Works*, vol. 4, *Sermon of the Conspiracy of the Gowries* 4, p. 77.

9. Ibid., p. 90.

10. *Works*, vol. 1, *Sermon of the Nativity* 1, pp. 10–11.

11. *Works*, vol. 2, *Sermon of the Resurrection* 1, pp. 201–202.

12. *Works*, vol. 2, *Sermon of the Resurrection* 6, pp. 286–87.

13. *Works*, vol. 3, *Sermon of the Sending of the Holy Ghost* 8, p. 255.

14. *Works*, vol. 4, *Sermon of the Gunpowder Treason* 1, p. 204.

15. Ibid., p. 211.

16. Ibid., p. 210.

17. Ibid., pp. 217–18.

18. *Works*, vol. 4, *Sermon of the Gunpowder Treason* 6, pp. 311–12.

19. *Works*, vol. 4, *Sermon of the Gunpowder Treason* 8, p. 352.

20. *Works*, vol. 4, *Sermon of the Gunpowder Treason* 2, p. 230.

21. *Works*, vol. 4, *Sermon of the Gunpowder Treason* 8, p. 347.

22. *Works*, vol. 4, *Sermon of the Gunpowder Treason* 7, pp. 325, 327, 330, 331.

23. Ibid., p. 334.

Chapter Ten

1. T. S. Eliot, *Selected Essays* (New York: Harcourt, Brace and Company, 1932; rpt. 1950), p. 301.

2. Andrewes's sense of loss at Hooker's death and his concern for Hooker's manuscripts are revealed in an interesting letter to Dr. Henry Parry: "I cannot choose but write though you do not: I never failed since I last saw you, but daily prayed for him till this very instant you sent this heavy news. I have hitherto prayed, *Serva nobis hunc:* now must I, *Da nobis alium*. Alas, for our great loss! and when I say ours, though I mean yours and mine, yet much more the common: with the less sense they have of so great a damage, the more sad we need to bewail them and ourselves, who know his works and his worth to be such as behind him he hath not (that I know) left any near him. . . . Good brother, have a care to deal with his executrix or executor, or (him that is like to have a great stroke in it) his father-in-law, that there be special care and regard for preserving such papers as he left, besides the three last books expected. By preserving I mean, that not only they be not embezzled, and come to nothing, but that they come not into great hands, who will only have use of them *quatenus et quousue,* and suppress the rest, or unhappily all: but rather into the hands of some of them that unfeignedly wished him well, though of the meaner sort . . . ." *Works,* vol. 11, *Letters of Bishop Andrewes,* pp. xl–xli.

3. Richard Hooker, *Of the Laws of Ecclesiastical Polity,* ed. Christopher Morris (London: Dent, Everyman's Library, 1907; rpt. 1969), I, 292.

4. Hooker, II, 54.

5. *Works,* vol. 7, *Tortura Torti,* p. 96, trans. Welsby, p. 149.

6. *Works,* vol. 9, *Opuscula Quaedam Posthuma, Concio Latine Habita in Discessu Palatini,* p. 91, trans. Maurice F. Reidy, S.J. in *Bishop Lancelot Andrewes* (Chicago: Loyola University Press, 1955), pp. 78–79.

7. Hooker, I, 268.

8. *Works,* vol. 3, *Sermon of the Sending of the Holy Ghost* 10, p. 287.

9. Hooker, I, 360.

10. *Works,* vol. 5, *Of the Worshipping of Imaginations,* p. 60.

11. Florence Higham, *Lancelot Andrewes* (London: SCM Press, 1952), p. 77.

12. *Andrewes: Seventeen Sermons on the Nativity* (London: Griffith, Farran, Okeden and Welsh, n.d.); and *John Donne: Sermons; Selected Passages,* ed. Logan Pearsall Smith (Oxford: Oxford University Press, 1919).

13. Eliot, p. 302.

14. Ibid., pp. 308, 309.

15. A useful comparison of the characteristics of Andrewes's and Donne's sermons is found in William R. Mueller, *John Donne: Preacher* (Princeton: Princeton University Press, 1962). Less extensive comparisons are found in Joan Webber, "Celebration of Word and World in Lancelot Andrewes' Style," in *Seventeenth-Century Prose: Modern Essays in Criticism,* ed. Stanley E. Fish (New York: Oxford University Press, 1971), and in Winfried Schleiner, *The Imagery of John Donne's Sermons* (Providence: Brown University Press, 1970).

16. Quoted by Eliot, p. 306.

17. *The Sermons of John Donne,* eds. George R. Potter and Evelyn M. Simpson (Berkeley and Los Angeles: University of California Press, 1962), II, 197.

18. *The Sermons of John Donne,* IV, 46–47.

19. *Works,* vol. 1, *Sermon of the Nativity* 9, p. 147.

20. Eliot, p. 307.

21. *The Works of Thomas Nashe,* ed. Ronald B. McKerrow (Oxford, 1904, rpt. Oxford: Basil Blackwell, 1958), III, 107.

22. John Aubrey, *Brief Lives,* ed. Oliver Lawson Dick (London: Secker and Warburg, 1949; rpt. Ann Arbor: University of Michigan Press, 1957), p. 7.

23. George Herbert, *A Priest to the Temple* (London, 1652) in *The Works of George Herbert,* 4th ed., ed. F. E. Hutchinson (Oxford: Clarendon Press, 1959), pp. 234–35.

24. Thomas Fuller, *Worthies,* cited by George Williamson in *The Senecan Amble: A Study in Prose Form from Bacon to Collier* (1951; rpt. Chicago: University of Chicago Press, Phoenix Books, 1966), p. 232, n.

25. Aubrey, p. 7.

26. Cited by Charles Smyth in *The Art of Preaching* (London: SPCK, 1940), p. 122.

27. Smyth, p. 106.

28. *The Complete Works of Samuel Taylor Coleridge,* ed. W. G. T. Shedd, *The Literary Remains* (New York: Harper and Brothers, 1871), V, 111, 112.

29. Alexander Whyte, *Lancelot Andrewes and His Private Devotions,* 2nd ed. (Edinburgh, 1896), pp. 16, 19.

30. F. E. Hutchinson, "The English Pulpit from Fisher to Donne," in *The Cambridge History of English Literature,* ed. A. W. Ward and A. R. Waller (New York: The Macmillan Company, 1910; rpt. 1939), IV, 274.

31. W. Fraser Mitchell, *English Pulpit Oratory from Andrewes to Tillotson* (London, 1932; rpt. New York: Russell and Russell, 1962), p. 194.

32. Maurice F. Reidy, S.J., *Bishop Lancelot Andrewes* (Chicago: Loyola University Press, 1955), pp. 53, 73.

33. Ibid., p. 218.

34. Joan Webber, "Celebration of Word and World in Lancelot Andrewes' Style," *Journal of English and Germanic Philology,* 64 (1965), rpt. in Stanley E. Fish, ed., *Seventeenth-Century Prose: Modern Essays in Criticism* (New York: Oxford University Press, 1971), p. 337.

35. Webber, p. 338.

36. Eliot, pp. 299, 302.

37. Ibid., p. 310.

38. Ibid., p. 299.

39. Kyle Haselden, *The Urgency of Preaching* (New York: Harper and Row, 1963), p. 26.

40. Works, vol. 1, *Epistle Dedicatory: To His Most Sacred Majesty Charles*, p. xiii.

41. *The Private Devotions of Lancelot Andrewes*, ed. F. E. Brightman (London: 1903; rpt. New York: Living Age Books, 1961), p. 254.

Selected Bibliography

PRIMARY SOURCES

The Works of Lancelot Andrewes, Sometime Bishop of Winchester. Ed. J. P. Wilson and James Bliss. 11 vols. Oxford: John Henry Parker, 1841–1854; rpt. New York: AMS Press, 1967. The first and only collected edition of all of Andrewes's works, published in the Library of Anglo-Catholic Theology Series. The volumes are as follows:

Volumes 1–5: *Ninety–Six Sermons By the Right Honourable and Reverend Father in God, Lancelot Andrewes*. Ed. J. P. Wilson. Oxford: John Henry Parker, 1841. The text of these sermons is printed from the second edition, published in 1632, collated with the 1641 and 1661 editions, and arranged as follows:

Volume 1: Seventeen Sermons of the Nativity and eight Sermons of Repentance and Fasting.

Volume 2: Six Sermons Preached in Lent, three Sermons of the Passion, and the first thirteen Sermons of the Resurrection.

Volume 3: The last five Sermons of the Resurrection and fifteen Sermons of the Sending of the Holy Ghost.

Volume 4: Eight Sermons of the Conspiracy of the Gowries and ten Sermons of the Gunpowder Treason.

Volume 5: Eleven Miscellaneous Sermons, A Sermon Preached Before Two Kings (not in the original group of Ninety-Six Sermons), the Sermon preached at Andrewes's funeral by John Buckeridge, nineteen Sermons Upon Prayer, and seven Sermons Upon the Temptation of Christ in the Wilderness. (These last two groups were not included in the original group of Ninety-Six Sermons.)

Volume 6: *A Pattern of Catechistical Doctrine and Other Minor Works of Lancelot Andrewes*. Oxford: John Henry Parker, 1846. In addition to the *Catechism*, this volume contains the *Judgment of the Lambeth Articles* (in Latin), the *Judgment of the Censure Upon Barret* (in Latin), the *Form of Consecration of a Church and Churchyard, A Summary View of the Government both of the Old and New Testament*, and *A Discourse of Ceremonies*.

Volume 7, *Tortura Torti*. Ed. James Bliss. Oxford: John Henry Parker, 1851.

Volume 8: *Responsio Ad Apologiam Cardinalis Bellarmini*. Ed. James Bliss. Oxford: John Henry Parker, 1851.

Volume 9: *Opuscula Quaedam Posthuma Lanceloti Andrewes*. Oxford: John Henry Parker, 1852. This volume contains seven of Andrewes's Latin Sermons, six of his Latin epistles to Peter Du Moulin (a French Hugenot), and a General Index to Andrewes's Latin Works.

Volume 10: *Preces Privatae Quotidianae Lanceloti Andrewes*. Ed. James Bliss. Oxford: John Henry Parker, 1853. This volume contains Andrewes's Private Greek and Latin Prayers.

Volume 11: *Two Answers to Cardinal Perron and other Miscellaneous Works*. Ed. James Bliss. Oxford: John Henry Parker, 1854. In addition to the *Answers to Cardinal Perron,* this volume contains Henry Isaacson's *Exact Narration of the Life and Death of . . . Lancelot Andrewes;* Sir John Harington's *Memoir of Bishop Andrewes;* eight of Andrewes's Letters; nine appendixes (including Andrewes's Will); *A Speech Delivered in the Starr-Chamber against . . . Mr. Traske; A Speech Delivered in the Starr-Chamber, Concerning Vowes, in the Countesse of Shrewsburies Case; A Disclosure Written . . . Against Second Marriage; Articles to be Enquired of by the Church-Wardens and Sworn-men* (1619 and 1625); *Notes on the Book of Common Prayer; A Coppie of the Forme Used . . . in Consecrating the Newe Church Plate; A Manual of Directions for the Sick; A Manual of the Private Devotions and Meditations*. (This work is the English translation made in 1648 by Richard Drake of Andrewes's *Preces Privatae*.) The eleventh volume concludes with an Index of Texts to Sermons and a General Index to Sermons and Minor Works.

Lancelot Andrewes: Sermons. Ed. G. M. Story. Oxford: Clarendon Press, 1967. An excellent anthology of twelve of the best of Andrewes's sermons. The collection, unlike the great nineteenth-century edition of the sermons, is based on the earliest printed editions (both the 1629 Folio and the quartos) with the original spellings. The introduction contains a concise biographical sketch and a good critical analysis of the sermons. A few factual errors appear in the introduction.

The Preces Privatae of Lancelot Andrewes. Trans. and ed. F. E. Brightman. London, 1903; rpt. New York: Living Age Books, 1961. The standard edition of Andrewes's *Private Devotions,* sensitively translated. The extremely valuable introduction not only illuminates the *Devotions* and the traditions behind them, but also provides an informative commentary on Andrewes's life and sermons.

SECONDARY SOURCES

1. Background of Andrewes's Age

BLENCH, J. W. *Preaching in England in the Late Fifteenth and Sixteenth Centuries*. New York: Barnes and Noble, 1964. A survey of English preaching from about 1450 through the sermons of Hooker and Andrewes, with emphasis on scriptural interpretation, form, style, the use of classical allusions, and themes.

FRERE, W. H. *The English Church in the Reigns of Elizabeth and James I (1558–1625)*. 1904; rpt. London: Macmillan and Company, 1924. A good background source on the English Church during Andrewes's lifetime.

HERR, ALAN FAGER. *The Elizabethan Sermon*. 1940; rpt. New York: Octagon Books, 1969. A concise survey of preaching in the Elizabethan age with a valuable bibliography.

HUTCHINSON, F. E. "The English Pulpit from Fisher to Donne." *The Cambridge History of English Literature*. Ed. A. W. Ward and A. R. Waller. New York: The Macmillan Company, 1910; rpt. 1939. Vol. 4, 257–77. A brief survey of English pulpit oratory of the sixteenth and earlier seventeenth centuries. The author is somewhat critical of Andrewes's preaching style.

KRAPP, GEORGE PHILIP. *The Rise of English Literary Prose*. 1915; rpt. New York: Frederick Ungar Publishing Company, 1963. Contains a valuable chapter on pulpit oratory from the later Middle Ages through the early seventeenth century with a good general discussion of Andrewes's stylistic characteristics.

MCADOO, H. R. *The Structure of Caroline Moral Theology*. London: Longmans, Green and Company, 1949. A concise introduction to the distinctively Anglican tradition of moral theology and piety, with references to Andrewes.

MCCLURE, MILLAR. *The Paul's Cross Sermons 1534–1642*. University of Toronto Department of English Studies and Texts, No. 6. Toronto: University of Toronto Press, 1958. A thorough study of the history of Saint Paul's Churchyard and the sermons preached there, especially helpful in its discussions of political themes in Elizabethan and Jacobean sermons.

MITCHELL, W. FRASER. *English Pulpit Oratory from Andrewes to Tillotson*. 1932; rpt. New York: Russell and Russell, 1962. The classic work in the field. A study of English pulpit oratory in the seventeenth century with an extensive discussion of the rhetorical background. This book thoroughly traces the development of "metaphysical" preaching from the late Elizabethan period through the reaction in the Restoration period with numerous examples. The author is not sympathetic to the "metaphysical" style of preaching.

SMYTH, CHARLES. *The Art of Preaching: A Practical Survey of Preaching in the Church of England 747–1939*. London: SPCK, 1940. A survey of English pulpit oratory from the beginnings to modern times, with good chapters on Andrewes's stylistic characteristics and the reaction against his style of preaching.

WILLIAMSON, GEORGE. *The Senecan Amble: A Study in Prose Form from Bacon to Collier*. 1951; rpt. Chicago: University of Chicago Press, Phoenix Books, 1966. A study of the Senecan style in the early seventeenth century and the reaction against it later in this century. The chapter "Scheme and Point in Pulpit Oratory" gives special attention to Andrewes's style of preaching.

Willson, David Harris. *King James VI and I*. London: Jonathan Cape, 1956. A good biography of Andrewes's patron, vividly presenting his personality and the atmosphere of his court. Several references to Andrewes and his relationship with the king.

2. Andrewes and His Works

Aubrey, John. *Brief Lives*. Ed. Oliver Lawson Dick. London: Secker and Warburg, 1949; rpt. Ann Arbor: University of Michigan Press, 1957. The "brief life" of Andrewes is composed mostly of three humorous anecdotes. It concludes with a brief, often-quoted criticism of Andrewes's preaching by an anonymous "Scotish Lord" who had heard him.

Bush, Douglas. *English Literature in the Earlier Seventeenth Century 1600–1660*. New York: Oxford University Press, 1945; rpt. 1952. Contains a conveniently concise discussion of Andrewes's style, somewhat unsympathetic.

Chamberlain, John. *Letters*. 2 vols. Ed. Norman Egbert McClure. Philadelphia: American Philosophical Society, 1939. Several references to Andrewes and his preaching, providing brief contemporary glimpses into his life.

Chambers, Douglas D. C. "Lancelot Andrewes and the Topical Structure of Thought." Unpublished doctoral dissertation, Princeton University, 1968. A specialized but valuable study of the influence of the traditions of logic and rhetoric on Andrewes's sermons. Contains an appendix listing Andrewes's library.

Church, Richard W. "Lancelot Andrewes." In *Masters of English Theology*, ed. Alfred Barry. London: John Murray, 1877. This work presents only a very general discussion of Andrewes's biography, preaching style, thought, and devotional life; it is mainly a panegyric to the Church of England.

Coleridge, Samuel Taylor. *The Complete Works*. Ed. W. G. T. Shedd. Vol. 5: *The Literary Remains*. New York: Harper and Brothers, 1871. Contains sympathetic praise for "our old divines": Hooker, Donne, and Andrewes.

Colville, Kenneth Newton. *Fame's Twilight: Studies of Nine Men of Letters*. London, 1923; rpt. Freeport, N.Y.: Books for Libraries Press, 1970. Contains a general discussion of Andrewes's life and prose style.

Eliot, T. S. *Selected Essays*. New York: Harcourt, Brace and Company, 1932; rpt. 1950. This collection contains Eliot's famous essay on Lancelot Andrewes written in 1926 to commemorate the three hundredth anniversary of his death. It provides a concise, perceptive description of the essential characteristics of Andrewes's style, contrasting his method with Donne's. This essay still remains the finest intoduction to Andrewes's achievement.

FOX, ARTHUR W. *A Book of Bachelors*. Westminster: Archibald Constable and Company, 1899. Discusses famous English bachelors. In the section entitled "The Bishop: Lancelot Andrewes," the author presents a general survey of Andrewes's biography, his roles as controversialist and preacher, and his prose style.

HIGHAM, FLORENCE. *Lancelot Andrewes*. London: SCM Press, 1952. Probably the most appealing of the Andrewes biographies, with several especially perceptive comments on his life and sermons. The biography, however, does contain some errors of fact which more recent studies have corrected.

MACLEANE, DOUGLAS. *Lancelot Andrewes and the Reaction*. London: George Allen and Sons, 1910. A convenient distillation of the basic facts of Andrewes's life, achievement, and reputation.

MCCUTCHEON, ELIZABETH. "Lancelot Andrewes and the Theme of Time in the Early Seventeenth Century." Unpublished doctoral dissertation, University of Wisconsin, 1961. A thorough discussion of the subject of time in Andrewes's writings and in other works of the seventeenth century, with thoughtful, sensitive comments on individual sermons. Especially interesting is the author's discovery of Andrewes's manuscript notes for one of his Pentecost sermons.

———. "Lancelot Andrewes' *Preces Privatae:* a Journey through Time." *Studies in Philology* 65 (April 1968): 223–41. Emphasizes the interrelationship between theme and form in Andrewes's *Private Devotions,* tracing in the morning prayers Andrewes's journey through time to eternity.

OTTLEY, ROBERT L. *Lancelot Andrewes*. London: Methuen and Company, 1894. Probably the best of the nineteenth-century studies of Andrewes. Presents a thorough survey of all the facets of Andrewes's life and work with especially helpful chapters on his role as controversialist.

REIDY, MAURICE F., S.J. *Bishop Lancelot Andrewes*. Chicago: Loyola University Press, 1955. This work deserves to be better known, since it provides the most thorough analysis by a modern writer of Andrewes's thought with numerous quotations from his writings. The writer, while recognizing greatness in groups of the sermons, is unsympathetic to Andrewes's prose style.

RUSSELL, ARTHUR T. *Memoirs of the Life and Works of the Right Honorable and Right Rev. Father in God Lancelot Andrewes*. Cambridge: J. Palmer, 1860. An unusually thorough discussion of Andrewes's life and work. The author, however, presents such a detailed survey of the background of Andrewes's age and the men with whom he came into contact that the study of Andrewes becomes tedious.

WEBBER, JOAN. "Celebration of Word and World in Lancelot Andrewes' Style." In *Seventeenth-Century Prose: Modern Essays in Criticism,* ed. Stanley E. Fish. New York: Oxford University Press, 1971. An excellent, concise, sympathetic analysis of Andrewes's prose style with a perceptive comparison of the characteristic methods of Andrewes and Donne.

WELSBY, PAUL A. *Lancelot Andrewes*. London: SPCK, 1958. The definitive biography. It painstakingly reconstructs the details of Andrewes's life from numerous, varied sources and it removes former errors of fact which had been passed down in previous biographies.

WHYTE, ALEXANDER. *Lancelot Andrewes and His Private Devotions*. 2nd ed. Edinburgh and London, 1896. This work in its introduction to a transcription of some of the *Devotions* presents a biography and discussion of Andrewes's sermons and *Devotions*. The author makes some pungent comments on Andrewes's life and the prose style of his sermons.

WILLIAMSON, HUGH ROSS. *Four Stuart Portraits*. London: Evans Brothers Limited, 1949. The "portrait" of Andrewes here is not the typical "saint's life"; instead it calls attention to weaknesses in Andrewes's character. Williamson is, apparently, the only writer on Andrewes's *Devotions* who is not enthusiastic about them; he declares that "their total effect is one almost of superficiality."

Index

DATE DUE
